Applying the Science of Six Sigma to the Art of Sales and Marketing

Also available from ASQ Quality Press:

Six Sigma Project Management: A Pocket Guide
Jeffrey N. Lowenthal

Six Sigma for the Office: A Pocket Guide
Roderick A. Munro

*Transactional Six Sigma for Green Belts: Maximizing Service and
 Manuacturing Processes*
Samuel E. Windsor

*Competing for Customers and Winning with Value: Breakthrough Strategies
 for Market Dominance*
R. Eric Reidenbach and Reginald W. Goeke

Defining and Analyzing a Business Process: A Six Sigma Pocket Guide
Jeffrey N. Lowenthal

*Applied Data Analysis for Process Improvement: A Practical Guide to Six
 Sigma Black Belt Statistics*
James L. Lamprecht

Word Success: Why and How to Express Yourself to the Good Life
Pete Geissler

Implementing Design for Six Sigma: A Leader's Guide
Georgette Belair and John O'Neill

*Everyday Excellence: Creating a Better Workplace through Attitude, Action,
 and Appreciation*
Clive Shearer

*The Certified Manager of Quality/Organizational Excellence Handbook:
 Third Edition*
Russell T. Westcott, editor

The Quality Toolbox, Second Edition
Nancy R. Tague

*Making Change Work: Practical Tools for Overcoming Human Resistance
 to Change*
Brien Palmer

To request a complimentary catalog of ASQ Quality Press publications, call
800-248-1946, or visit our Web site at http://qualitypress.asq.org.

Applying the Science of Six Sigma to the Art of Sales and Marketing

Michael J. Pestorius

ASQ Quality Press
Milwaukee, Wisconsin

American Society for Quality, Quality Press, Milwaukee 53203
© 2007 ASQ
All rights reserved. Published 2006
Printed in the United States of America

12   11   10   09   08   07   06   5 4 3 2 1

Library of Congress Cataloging-in-Publication Data

Pestorius, Michael J.
  Applying the Science of Six Sigma to the art of sales and marketing / Michael J.
Pestorius.
      p. cm.
   ISBN-13 978- 0-87389-696-2
   1. Sales managment. 2. Selling. 3. Six sigma (Quality control standard) I. Title.

HF5438.4.P467 2006
658.8'101—dc22

                                                                    2006025825

Publisher: William A. Tony
Acquisitions Editior: Matt Meinholz
Project Editor: Paul O'Mara
Production Administrator: Randy Benson

ASQ Mission: The American Society for Quality advances individual,
organization, and community excellence worldwide through learning,
quality improvement, and knowledge exchange.

Attention Bookstores, Wholesalers, Schools and Corporations: ASQ Quality Press
books, videotapes, audiotapes, and software are available at quantity discounts
with bulk purchases for business, education, or instructional use.
For information, please contact ASQ Quality Press at 800-24801946, or write to
ASQ Quality PRess, P.O. Box 3005, Milwaukee, WI 53201-3005.

To place orders or to request a free copy of the ASQ Quality PRess Publication
Catalog, including ASQ membership information, call 800-248-1946. Visit our
Web site at www.asq.org or http://qualitypress.asq.org.

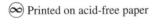 Printed on acid-free paper

Quality Press
600 N. Plankinton Avenue
Milwaukee, Wisconsin 53203
Call toll free 800-248-1946
Fax 414-272-1734
www.asq.org
http://qualitypress.asq.org
http://standardsgroup.asq.org
E-mail: authors@asq.org

Dedication

This book is dedicated to everyone who helped make it possible. Thanks to Steven Jackson and Tom McFarland for their advice, support and editorial expertise. Thank you for the guidance and understanding of ASQ and the input of my reviewer team, especially David Foxx. I am also grateful to the multiple Six Sigma professionals with whom I have had the pleasure to work, especially Mark Gardner, Joe Magro, Jeff Naglestad, Thom Fish, and many other individuals too numerous to list.

Finally I would like to thank my wife, Cara. She gave me the encouragement and support to complete this and possessed the understanding and patience required to endure the trial of getting this book written, edited, and published. She and our children have my deepest gratitude and love.

Contents

List of Figures
and Tables

Preface

Six Sigma is a highly flexible methodology and tool set, but few practitioners have successfully transferred the early successes Six Sigma enjoyed in manufacturing to sales and marketing. The opportunities to use it exist, but the expertise on how to apply it is lacking.

This book provides step-by-step instructions on how to use data and measures to tackle common business challenges. An analysis of the territory planning process provides tools and techniques to improve the effectiveness of salesforces that suboptimize their efforts by calling on the wrong customers. It shows sales leadership how to use readily available data to ensure that the "right" customers are receiving the attention they need. It also quantifies the real cost of spending time with customers that are not improving the bottom line.

A historical analysis of product promotions takes the guesswork out of developing future sales campaigns. This is accomplished by taking the time to define a specific goal and develop metrics that will allow side-by-side evaluations of the effectiveness of past promotions. Once armed with this knowledge, future promotions stand a greater chance of achieving their goals.

Other chapters cover projects on improving product launch sales, improving the effectiveness of the sales rep/sales manager field-visit process, sale representative hiring profiles and sale representative training. Ultimately this book is intended to provide answers to those who question the applicability of Six Sigma in Sales and Marketing.

Ultimately, this book answers those who are skeptical about the usefulness of Six Sigma in sales and marketing. It addresses these skeptics with step by step instructions on how to apply Six Sigma to common sales and marketing challenges.

If management is willing to apply the same rigor and measurement to sales and marketing processes as are applied to other business processes, then sales leadership can refine their focus and improve the returns on for their efforts.

Introduction

"You cannot open a book without learning something."

Confucius

Since its introduction at Motorola in the late 1980's, Six Sigma has assumed multiple aliases—these include: Operations Excellence, Business Process Improvement, and Process Excellence. Regardless of the moniker used, the goal of Six Sigma companies has remained consistent: to encourage continuous process improvement by utilizing a standardized, documented, and repeatable problem solving methodology.

Six Sigma provides a common language and method to address business opportunities and solve business problems. It provides a roadmap that guides problem solvers where to start and what to do next. Although common tools and language are utilized, Six Sigma is flexible enough to be applied to different challenges throughout business, wherever they may arise—manufacturing, finance, procurement, sales, marketing, or any other functional area. The five common steps for applying Six Sigma are captured in the acronym "DMAIC". DMAIC stands for Define, Measure, Analyze, Improve, and Control. These five simple steps have driven incredible results at thousands of companies.

During the Define phase of a Six Sigma project, issues are accurately and precisely defined, the scope of the work is determined, and the metrics that will track the progress of improvement are identified. The Measure phase sees the collection and preliminary analysis of the data that describes the process. The Analyze phase focuses on identifying the underlying causes of the problem or the key driver of an opportunity. During the Improve phase, the effectiveness of improvement is tested. Finally, during the Control phase, the improved process is fully integrated back into the business and safeguards are set into place to ensure that it does not regress back to the state that required the initial improvement effort.

Since the earliest adoptions of Six Sigma, there has been an unfortunate but common perception that Six Sigma can only improve pure manufacturing processes, and that a fact-based problem solving methodology does not transfer well to transactional processes, specifically in sales and marketing. This attitude is especially common among many sales and marketing professionals. Most of the non-believers question the ability and effectiveness of applying a standardized problem solving method to the "art" of sales and marketing. They believe that theirs is such a dynamic and sometimes nebulous environment that a structured approach requiring processes, metrics, and data would only hinder the creative magic that is required to be successful. This is simply not the case. Six Sigma does not suppress creativity; rather it provides a framework to channel it. Just as a painter's creativity is revealed in a finished work, he does not protest standard paints, brushes, or canvas. Six Sigma provides practical guidance on how to begin the process of solving a problem and provides questions to ask along the way. Creativity flourishes in the content and throughput of a successful solution, not necessarily in the tools uses to achieve the outcome. Six Sigma is the engine that drives results; creativity is the fuel. Practitioners of Six Sigma, especially those that truly understand and embrace the concept, are confident that it is indeed appropriate and extremely useful in unlocking the enormous potential benefit in refined sales and marketing processes.

Although Six Sigma has been very popular in manufacturing for over a decade, sales and marketing leaders have only recently started to utilize it. This delayed appreciation is the result of four main factors: the facility with which Six Sigma can be applied to manufacturing processes, the background of most Six Sigma professionals, the relative strength in consumer purchasing over the last several years, and existing sales culture.

In most manufacturing processes, almost every variable can be precisely controlled. Reducing defects and improving efficiency is already ingrained into the psyche and culture. Manufacturing facilities provide fertile soil for the application of problem-solving methods that focus on measuring processes and tight control of input variables to achieve optimal outcomes. Forerunners of Six Sigma, such as statistical process control (SPC), Total Quality Management (TQM) and ISO 9000 methodologies, have been used for years in manufacturing settings. In fact, one of the primary drivers of the American industrial revolution was the ability to mass produce relatively defect free products. The process efficiency efforts of Henry Ford and Alfred Sloan at General Motors allowed their companies separate themselves from their competition to become industrial giants. Unfortunately, their more recent inability to maintain efficiency parity with their competitors has been a seed of their downfall.

A second element that has hindered the spread of Six Sigma into sales and marketing is the background of most Six Sigma professionals. For years, the majority of Six Sigma professionals hailed from manufacturing. These individuals are often less familiar with transactional processes and may not recognize the potential for applying Six Sigma there. This lack of understanding is significant, since to successfully apply Six Sigma one must be familiar with both the Six Sigma tools and the environment in which they are being applied. After all, an auto mechanic would certainly feel more comfortable using a new set of pliers in a garage than in an operating room, even though the tool is appropriate in both environments.

The third factor that may have slowed the application of Six Sigma to transactional processes has been the relative strength in consumer purchasing patterns in the last few years. In order for a company to dedicate itself to any improvement effort, there must be a strong cause for action. Manufacturing had that cause for action. The globalization of the world economy has removed barriers of entry for low cost manufacturers into established markets. These new entrants competed directly with established manufacturers. These new, low-cost, high-quality competitors forced traditional manufacturers to search for opportunities to improve their operations. The result of this increased competition was a commensurate increase in the supply of most products at reduced prices. As captured in the figure below, this upward shift in supply and downward shift in price drove additional demand—therefore sales increased across multiple industries.

This increase in sales drove record revenues that masked any need for improved sales and marketing efficiencies. Fat bottom lines drove many sales and marketing professionals to ask: "why should we worry about process improvements while sales and revenue are increasing at record

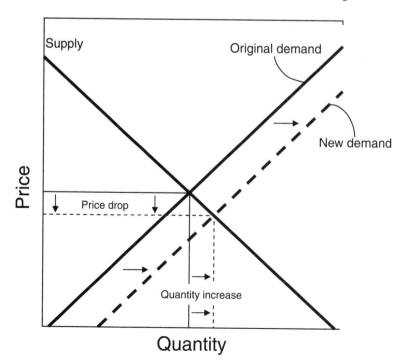

levels?" This attitude, though logically achieved, prevented the arrival of the required cause for action in sales and marketing. Interestingly, this same logic originally delayed Six Sigma in many manufacturing environments.

The final element that stymied the growth of Six Sigma in sales and marketing was the existing sales culture. This entrepreneurial spirit actively resists standardized processes and encourages independence and freedom. If Six Sigma is misconstrued as negatively impacting this spirit, it will be opposed.

Applying Six Sigma requires altering both processes and attitudes. When everything seems to be working well, it is difficult to convince people that change is needed. Only recently have many CEOs started to investigate the potential for trying to apply Six Sigma to non-manufacturing processes.

This book is intended to provide a brief overview of Six Sigma and present several examples of how Six Sigma can be applied to transactional processes. This book is not intended to teach the Six Sigma methodology or even sell its utility. By purchasing this book, you have already declared your belief in the value of Six Sigma and its potential benefit to sales and marketing processes. This book covers the DMAIC approach exclusively. Lean, DFSS (Design for Six Sigma), and DMADV (Define, Measure, Analyze, Design, Verify) are also very useful and popular process improvement methodologies, but outside the scope of this book. The examples presented cover a spectrum of Six Sigma tools and applications. Some of the examples in this book are classic Six Sigma projects that closely follow each step of the DMAIC process. Some are not "projects" but are rather the application of Six Sigma tools to common sales and marketing challenges.

This is not a statistics book. Some common statistics tools are used, but this is by no means intended to be the authoritative guide on which statistical tools to use in specific situations. Oftentimes, multiple statistical tools can be applied to any particular problem. The ones utilized here are the choices of the author.

The intended purpose of this book is to simply answer the question: "Where can Six Sigma be successfully applied in sales and marketing?"

1

The Evolution of Six Sigma

U tilizing Six Sigma to improve business processes evolved from shop floor applications of statistical process control to the current state of applying processes and measures to all business processes. This progression can be perceived as advancing through three main stages, with the third stage currently underway. The genesis of Six Sigma, and, in the opinion of many, still the most fertile soil, in terms of ease of application, is in manufacturing. Manufacturing facilities are usually led by engineers who are inherently familiar with the DMAIC concept—whether they have been formally trained or not. There is little need to convince them of the advantage of tracking defects back to their sources; trying to identify the root causes of failure, and then implementing a controlled solution. Other factors that have facilitated the success of Six Sigma in manufacturing, other than those already discussed, include:

1. Defects in a manufacturing process are usually obvious, such as a busted widget or a machine that doesn't work. Obvious problems often have obvious solutions. Even if the solution is not obvious, it is usually easy to gain the support needed to launch an effort to eliminate the defect.

2. Relatively short manufacturing cycle times can quickly validate or invalidate process improvements. If a machine produces 500 parts per day and a certain percentage of them are defective, any improvement to the process can be quickly authenticated. On the other hand, improvements to a sales process may take months to produce measurable results.

3. A final advantage for Six Sigma practitioners in the manufacturing environments is that a majority of the variables that impact the processes are controllable. A plant manager can control his vendors,

the speeds of conveyer belts, the RPM, of drills, and the temperature of ovens. Since all of these process inputs can be so closely controlled, a manufacturing Six Sigma Black Belt or Master Black Belt[1] can achieve very precise improvements. For example, if the owner of a bakery started receiving complaints about cookies being burned, he could easily follow each step of the manufacturing process to determine the root cause of the problem. Once the root cause was identified, the oven was too hot, the baker could modify the process—reduce the temperature of the oven—and future defects would be averted. Unfortunately, few transactional processes are so straightforward or as easily controlled.

As business leaders became aware of the improvements Six Sigma was driving in manufacturing, they rushed to apply it to other business functions in hopes of reaping similar benefits. The next logical place for Six Sigma was in other data-rich environments that mirror manufacturing's need for repeatable processes minimal defects. This led to its introduction of Six Sigma into finance and information management. The finance department requires a robust and defect-free process to effectively close the books, pay royalties, track expenses, and pay salaries and commissions. The recent introduction of Sarbanes-Oxley regulations mandate documented, repeatable financial processes. The opportunities to optimize these processes have resulted in the recent embrace of Six Sigma by multiple financial service companies, including Bank of America, Merrill Lynch, and American Express. Imagine the money and effort that could be saved if the finance department could accurately close the quarter in a few days versus two weeks.

Information management also needs robust processes to efficiently and effectively provide software, deliver hardware, and manage data. Six Sigma provides tools to help accomplish these tasks.

Finance and information management are usually led and staffed by process-oriented individuals who recognize and appreciate the advantages of standardized processes. Six Sigma has fulfilled this need for structure in both functions. Hundreds of books have been dedicated to the application of Six Sigma in manufacturing, information management, and finance. Thousands of Green Belts, Black Belts, and Master Black Belts[1] call these functions "home." The first two steps in the evolution of Six Sigma from manufacturing to finance and information management are well established.

The third, and ongoing, step in the evolution of Six Sigma is its application to transactional process, most notably in sales and marketing. This has proven to be the most difficult stage in the growth of Six Sigma as a cross-functional application. Some of the reasons for this challenge are in

---

[1] The colors of belts indicate Six Sigma expertise and capability. Green Belt is the most basic Six Sigma certification while Master Black Belt is the most advanced.

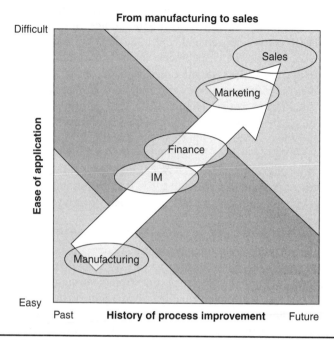

Figure 1.1 The evolution of Six Sigma.

identifying appropriate projects and driving the culture shift that is required for transactional leaders to embrace the concept. Driving this change is difficult, but worth pursuing. The potential savings that can be realized from improved transactional processes is significant because, unlike most manufacturing efficiency gains, improved sales processes directly impact top line sales and therefore bottom-line profit. Unfortunately, a lack of precise control over many of the variables in transactional processes has restricted the use of Six Sigma. There is an approximate inverse relationship between the ease of application of Six Sigma and potential savings it can drive.

As previously noted, it is fairly simple to apply Six Sigma to classical manufacturing processes due to the relative transparency of those processes and the ability to control most of the variables. However, years of manufacturing process refinements have eliminated most "low-hanging fruit." On the other hand, there is a lot of "low hanging fruit" to be found in poorly controlled sales and marketing processes. It is this very lack of control that has allowed, and driven, the wide variation that exists in so many transactional processes. If this variation were easy to control, it would have already been done; but controlling sales and marketing processes is inherently more difficult than fixing manufacturing or finance processes. Unlike in manufacturing, the most important and least controllable variable in transactional processes is the human element.

In a manufacturing process, many of the process steps are automated and, once set, free of excessive human interference. Since these steps can usually be precisely adjusted and controlled, it is not unusual to achieve very high correlations[2] between process inputs to the quality of the process outputs. Human activities, on the other hand, are far less controllable or predictable. Therefore, processes that require high human input eschew control. The linkages between inputs and outputs are simply not as easy to adjust as they are in manufacturing processes. Additionally, in sales and marketing processes many important variables such as customers, competitors, and the weather are completely uncontrollable, but have a huge impact on process outcomes. Acknowledging these challenges should not be construed as reason to abandon the idea that Six Sigma can work in this environment—it is just recognition of the reality that fewer process variables are controllable.

Six Sigma should simply be applied to those variables that *can* be controlled. This may not lead to the near-perfect correlations that are seen in manufacturing projects, but correlations of over 50 to 60 percent[3] can still be achieved. This provides strong directional accuracy that was not available prior to the implementation of Six Sigma. In a world where 20 percent margins and 10 percent growth is considered successful, making critical decisions with 50 or 60 percent certainty, rather than 0 percent is an enormous and profitable improvement.

---

[2] Correlation is the degree or extent of the relationship between two variables. If the value of one variable increases when the value of the other increases, they are said to be positively correlated. If the value of one variable decreases when the value other variable is increasing it is said to be negatively correlated. If one variable does not affect the other they are not correlated.

[3] Correlation is measured by a variable known as the Pearson's correlation coefficient. This figure reflects the degree of linear relationship between two variables. Pearson's correlation coefficient (r) for continuous (interval level) data ranges from -1 to $+1$. A measure of $+1$ would indicate perfectly positive correlation. A measure of -1 would indicate perfectly negative correlation.

2

The Myth That Six Sigma Is Only for Operations

S ix Sigma critics often recite the common mantra: "Six Sigma concepts and tools can only be applied to manufacturing environments and will not transfer well into the transactional arena." They will question the time commitments required to apply the DMAIC methodology to problems. For each critic, there needs to be a convert to discover the root of skepticism. The easy questions to ask are:

- "Why don't you believe it will work?"

- "Do you think there is not enough data in a transactional environment for Six Sigma to work?"

- "Are your sales or marketing processes so strong that they cannot be improved?"

- "Are you concerned that the people who work in these areas do not have the intellectual bandwidth, desire, or willingness to deal with the slight amount of math that some Six Sigma projects require?"

The answers to these questions generally expose prejudices about the value of Six Sigma and how it is applied, but they rarely reveal fact-based reasons for rejection. At its core, Six Sigma is all about finding the root cause of a problem and solving it. The same approach should be applied to finding the root cause of skepticism toward applying it to transactional processes. Efficient sales and marketing processes are critically important to business; a defined approach to solving problems there can pay remarkable dividends.

Sales and marketing are closer to customers than any other business function and generate the fuel on which businesses run — cash. Meeting customers' desires should be a company's single most important task. Figure 2.1 illustrates some of these important linkages. Meeting customer desires

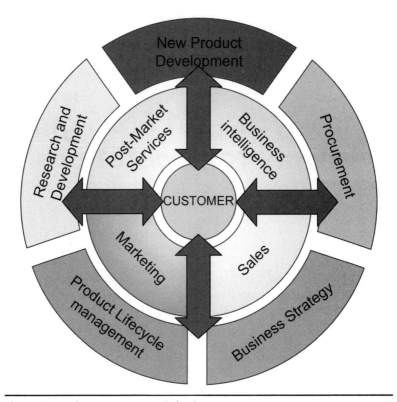

Figure 2.1 The customer centric business.

should drive the overall strategy of every business. It should determine what a company should make and sell.

Customer desires impact *where* companies will make and sell their products, and *how* they will make and sell them. Sales tell companies what to make next as well as what to stop making. Customer buying patterns help determine price points and what manufacturing materials should be used. Customer input defines much of the work of research and development groups. Procurement divisions exist to find raw materials to build products that meet customers' specifications. Distribution's overriding responsibility is to ensure that customers get the products they want, where they want them, and when they want them.

A company that is unaware of or ignores customer desires will suffer and ultimately perish. This demise can occur two ways: either the customer tells a company what to do and the company cannot "hear" their customers or, even if a company has the ability to "hear" the customers, it simply ignores what they are saying. Initiating this back-and-forth dialogue with customers to understand their needs is the primary responsibility of marketing departments. Isn't it logical that such important decisions and data are captured and analyzed with some rigor? A customer-centric business is one that makes every critical sales and marketing decision based on how that decision will ultimately impact its customers. The value of this customer feedback is priceless.

BUT THERE IS NOT ENOUGH DATA . . .

The transactional environment is filled with data; sales data, market data, territory data, sales representative data, and customer data. Sales and marketing professionals are constantly pursuing market data and competitive intelligence to determine how well they are fulfilling their customers' unmet needs, how well they are penetrating new environments, and the impact of newly launched products on sales, revenue, customers, and competitors. Six Sigma provides the roadmap to capture, analyze, and foster decisions based on this data.

OUR SALES PROCESSES ARE ALREADY STRONG . . .

Having a customer choose to pay for your product or service over a competitor's product is the ultimate goal of any sales or marketing organization. This purchase is the ultimate throughput of multiple process steps, some controllable and some not. Even a slight improvement in the effectiveness of a few of these controllable process steps will lead to the improved throughput of the process. Figure 2.2 describes a generic five-step sales process. The ultimate effectiveness of the process is calculated by multiplying the effectiveness of each step – this calculation is called a *rolled throughput yield* (RTY).

The RTY is analogous to the efficiency of a bucket brigade — a chain of people working to put out a fire by passing buckets of water from person to person. Imagine there are five people in the chain and each one spills 10 percent of the water from the bucket as they pass it to the next person. Therefore each person is 90 percent efficient at transporting the water. At the end of the chain, when the water is to be thrown on the fire, the bucket that started out full will have lost quite a bit of water. The efficiency of the bucket brigade is calculated by multiplying the efficiencies of each member of the team.

$$0.90 \times 0.90 \times 0.90 \times 0.90 \times 0.90 = .591$$

Even though each individual is 90 percent effective, the whole team is collectively only 59 percent efficient; 41 percent of the water is wasted.

The RTY of the sales process in Figure 2.2 can be similarly calculated. The RTY also shows how a large overall process improvement can be driven

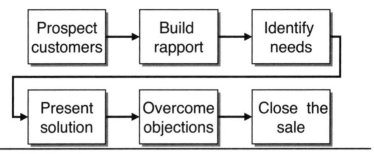

Figure 2.2 The sales process.

by driving only slight improvements to individual process steps. If a sales representative is 90 percent efficient at each step in the 5-step process, at the end of the process the sales representative will be successful 59 percent of the time. If the sales rep is able to improve their efficiency by only 5 percent per process step, to 95 percent, the RTY of the process will improve to

$$0.95 \times 0.95 \times 0.95 \times 0.95 \times 0.95 = .774$$

Just a slight improvement to each step in the sales process has improved sales from 59 percent to 77 percent, an improvement by over 18 percent. If a sales process were previously generating $1 million, this level of improvement would result in an additional $180,000.

If common, end-to-end process steps are closely observed, documented, and studied, and if the data they produce are collected and analyzed, it is possible to identify improvement opportunities within the process. The newly refined process can become a competitive advantage. Once the "science" of the sales process is identified and documented, more effort can be applied to refining the "art" of the sale.

WHERE CAN SIX SIGMA BE APPLIED IN SALES AND MARKETING?

There are multiple opportunities to improve sales and marketing processes. Clearly, selling a product to a customer is certainly the most important process in sales and marketing. This is an obvious area to focus Six Sigma efforts, but not the only area. There are several subordinate processes that support the selling process. Many of these processes, such as ordering samples or sales literature, are consistent across a salesforce and could potentially be standardized. Any of these processes could be studied and refined in order to optimize the end-to-end sales process. Some additional sales processes that may provide opportunities to utilize Six Sigma include:

- Interviewing and hiring successful sales representatives

- Training sales representatives on both the sales process and the various products and services about which they are expected to be experts
- Defining the most efficient way to manage a sales representative's samples stock
- Identifying and nurturing the most profitable customers and territories out of all the opportunities
- Getting marketing materials through copy review

These are common processes that both sales and marketing groups need to focus on in order to be successful. None of them require the "magic" of relationship building or personal charisma; they just require rigor.

"BANDWIDTH" CONCERNS

Some have insinuated that one of the reasons that salespeople avoid Six Sigma is because it is "too hard." It is an insult to insinuate that sales and marketing professionals do not have the capability to handle the Six Sigma methodology or the limited math it may require. This simply does not reflect the profile of a successful salesperson.

The financial rewards from a successful sales career are significantly higher than most other professions. The fruits of a successful sales career create competition for those roles. In a competitive market, sales professionals would not be able to achieve success without strong intellectual capacity. These financial rewards inspire many of the "best and the brightest" to pursue careers in business, as opposed to law, medicine, or science. In several industries, first-year sales professionals can out-earn first-year engineers, doctors, or lawyers. Successful sales professionals can maintain this lead throughout their careers.

The perceived complexity of Six Sigma is not the reason why it has not been successful in sales and marketing. The primary reason Six Sigma has not been widely introduced there is unwillingness of sales and marketing leadership to embrace the methodology.

The people involved in transactional processes are often unwilling to adopt a measurement-based methodology in a business function that they see as being driven purely by relationships and the strength of their personalities. Adopting Six Sigma represents change, and people do not like change, especially change that seems counterintuitive to what has worked for them in the past. There may be a concern that the attributes and capabilities that have fueled past success may not be useful in a Six Sigma environment—skills such as relationship building, creativity, and market knowledge. Salespeople may fear that a lack of math acumen will be exposed during Six Sigma training. These fears are common, but unfounded.

Anyone who is able to navigate a successful sales career is equally capable of not only handling but also mastering Six Sigma, regardless of what they studied in college. It is also worth mentioning that very little statistics or math is actually required to employ Six Sigma. Many of the most useful Six Sigma tools are very simple—such as a process map or a prioritization matrix. Both of these tools can drive significant process improvement and do not require any statistics. The statistical tools that Six Sigma uses are basic and have been successfully taught to millions of nonstatisticians and the math-phobic. Even though there are plenty of very complex statistical tools one can apply, the simple ones usually provide sufficient answers. This is analogous to the tools a carpenter has at his disposal. He can certainly produce great results with laser guides, pneumatic nail guns, and electric compound miter saws, but he can also achieve great results with a hammer, a screwdriver, and a pair of vise-grips. The judicious use of simple tools can produce great results.

So far, we have discussed some of the academic aspects of Six Sigma. Now it is time to introduce real-life examples of how to apply it to sales and marketing.

3

Sales Rep Hiring Profile

Imagine that two candidates present themselves at a job interview. One is brilliant, with deep technical knowledge. Unfortunately, their previous job reviews and interview behavior do not reveal any hint of ambition, friendliness, compassion, or courage. The second candidate's technical acumen is not nearly as strong, but she quickly engages the interviewer with charm and glowing relationship-building skills. Her past performance and experiences indicate strong leadership, optimism in the face of adversity, and deep curiosity. Regardless of the finishing schools that the first candidate could attend, he will probably never possess a fraction of the personality of the second candidate, but will always be technically superior. On the other hand, if the second candidate is sent to product training, she may be able to achieve sufficient technical acumen to succeed at the job. Which candidate should be hired? The tale of these two candidates leads to the central question: "What are the predictors of sales success?"

A standard comment throughout sales and marketing organizations is: "Great sales representatives are born, not made." We do not intend to debate this philosophy, but rather to test it.

If this nature/nurture argument is to be accepted, then it should be equally applicable to any other occupation. Any profession could repeat the comment: "Great (*fill in vocation*) are born, not made." In almost any line of work some individuals seem to naturally display specific talents that facilitate their success. An eye for detail is just as important to an accountant as speed is to a world-class sprinter. Both talents are so ingrained that they cease to be technical capabilities but are actually personality traits, which can only be refined, not taught. Table 3.1 provides examples of each.

Whether great sales representatives are born or made, the great ones seem to share similar qualities. If these capabilities are indeed personality traits and not technical skills, then these traits have been part of their composition most of their lives. If these champions' traits are common, then their past performances in other fields, such as academics, athletics, or leadership, may also be common. Since technical skills can be taught, they are not

Table 3.1   Talents that ensure success in any profession.

Personality traits	Technical capabilities
Curiosity	Math skills
Emotional strength	Selling skills
Friendliness	Language skills
Ambition	Product knowledge

as critical to the hiring profile as personality traits. Personality traits, on the other hand, cannot be taught with any more success than a basketball coach can "teach" a player to be tall. Therefore, their technical personality traits should be more heavily weighted capabilities when making hiring decisions. Technical skills are still important, just not *as* important.

If a job candidate arrives without some specific technical skill, but possesses personality traits that have proven to lead to success, that applicant should be strongly considered for the job; the required technical skills can be acquired later. These candidates may take longer to achieve profitability while they "learn the ropes" but their long-term success will be far greater.

Too often, sales representatives are hired based on the gut feel, and not on any specific, measurable success factors. It is common knowledge that, without intervention, hiring managers will generally hire people with whom they feel most comfortable. This leads to managers hiring people most like themselves. Hopefully then, the hiring manager is, or was, a great sales representative. Hopefully, that manager will hire great sales representatives— but a company shouldn't base its future and its face to its customers on gut feel and luck, even if it has worked a few times in the past.

Companies envision success for every candidate they hire; otherwise an employment offer would have never been extended. How many of these new hires did not turn out as they were envisioned? Wouldn't it have been useful to have some proactive measure of their potential success before they entered the salesforce? When sales reps are unsuccessful, all of the effort that was expended to hire them has been wasted. All of the money spent to recruit, train, and compensate them becomes a sunk cost that cannot be recovered. Additionally, the long process of replacing them must be repeated. The impact of this failure is felt both inside and outside of the company; in damage to the company's reputation and customer relationships. A bad rep can damage sales long after having been replaced. This is because a bad sales representative can damage the reputation of an *entire* company. Reputations that took years to build can be lost in the blink of an eye. Additionally, there is the opportunity cost of "what could have been" if a competent rep had been hired in the first place. This cost of a bad hire can be even higher and last longer if customer relationships have been damaged through untoward or illegal behavior.

Regardless of what a company sells, their market is probably becoming more competitive. A company needs consistently great products and consistently great sales representatives to be successful. The metrics that define this greatness need to be defined and tracked. The salesforce is a company's face to its customers; such an important element of success should not be selected without some significant thought behind the process.

DEFINE

The goal of this project is to identify the common indicators of great sales representatives and create a model to recruit the next generation of champions. This is obviously an important topic that sales leaders have thought about at length, but has a comprehensive study been undertaken to apply some rigor to the process? In the past, would human resources be solely responsible for this type of project? To gain traction and acceptance, this project needs to be led by a strong sponsor/champion from sales.

One of the most important elements in this project is to accurately define "success." What defines a "good" sales representative? Do not immediately assume that the best measure of success is revenue produced, units sold, or forecast achievement. These are certainly important metrics, but are they the best ones? Is a sales representative who constantly cuts price in order to move product more or less successful than one with strong pricing discipline? Market growth and speed to profitability should also be considered when defining success. Perhaps turnover has been an issue, so longevity may become part of the overall success metric. Regional factors may impact some representatives more severely than others. A great representative may be fighting the toughest competition in the country, but is still driving growth, though not as quickly as some of his less capable peers. Unfortunately, this success may be overlooked due to existing measures. A mediocre rep may be having a great sales year due to some reason other than inherent capabilities, such as a selling against a competitor's empty territory. It is incumbent on the project team to recognize these situations and account for them. Therefore, excellence must be defined so that success, regardless of the territory in which it is achieved, is accurately identified and tracked. One suggestion is to use the sales growth of a new representative or a new territory. How quickly can a new representative change the sales trend of an existing territory? Another suggestion is to identify multiple success characteristics. This way, single variables will not overtly impact an overall evaluation.

The ultimate success metric is probably a combination of factors. For example, a successful rep may be defined as one who remains in his or her territory for more than three years and is over plan at least 75 percent of the time. There is not one universally "correct" metric, so it is important to consider all potential factors when identifying the "best" sales representatives.

This project team has decided to measure success as sales growth during the first year of daily sales activity. Since it takes several months for new-hires to learn their way around their territories, the project team will not start collecting data until the sale representatives have been in their territory for six months. This will help to mitigate any lingering effects, either good or bad, of the previous occupant. Additionally, to lessen the effects of any truly "special case" territories, only the middle 90 percent of the data will be used; that is, the top and bottom 5 percent of the accounts will not be considered. This may cause the project to exclude some potentially strong performers, but since any significant outliers could skew the entire project, it is an acceptable risk to ignore those. Since they only represent 10 percent of the entire population, they can be investigated individually.

The "define" phase also calls for a high-level process map. Figure 3.1 uses a SIPOC (Suppliers, Inputs, Process, Outputs, Customers) to illustrate the process.

The SIPOC is a very useful tool when discussing or documenting independent or linked processes. If a company has effectively linked its critical processes—marketing to sales for instance—every output of one process should become an input to another process, just as every pitcher needs a catcher. This chain of input to output to input to output should continue until the customer takes final ownership of the product.

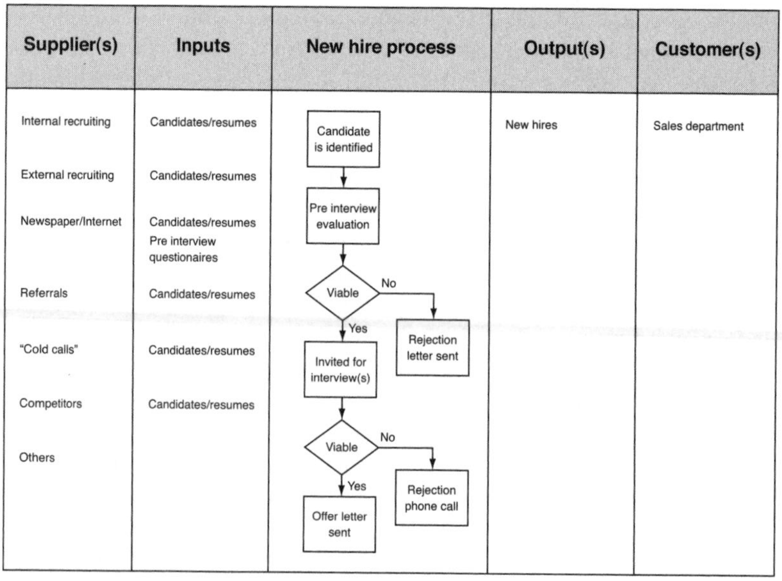

Figure 3.1 New hire process.

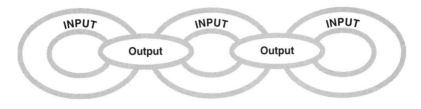

Figure 3.2 Linked processes.

If a process "output" is left dangling, then what is its value? Why is it being created if it is not feeding another process? This vision of process linkages makes the SIPOC a powerful but simple tool that can quickly uncover process efficiencies.

An SIPOC is not intended to show every intimate detail of the end-to-end process. Its purpose is to present a simple, high-level view of the process that is being considered and to list any required inputs and outputs. This initial process view may be modified as the process becomes better defined through the Six Sigma project progresses.

MEASURE

"I often say that when you can measure what you are speaking about and express it in numbers, you know something about it; but when you cannot express it in numbers, your knowledge is of a meager and unsatisfactory kind. It may be the beginning of knowledge but you have scarcely, in your thoughts, advanced to a state of science, whatever the matter may be."

Lord Kelvin (1883)

In some transactional projects, acquiring sufficient data may present a challenge. That should not be a problem in this project. It is said, "What is important is measured." Sales are important, ergo, they are measured. If this data is not available, a data collection plan that clearly identifies the required data and how to collect it should be developed and launched. If there is any question about the accuracy of the data, the measurement system should be evaluated. Six Sigma provides a strong method for evaluation measurement systems. It is outside of the scope of this book, but should be within the purview of a capable Black Belt.[1]

---

[1] Black Belts are Six Sigma team leaders responsible for implementing process improvement projects. They are knowledgeable and skilled in the use of the Six Sigma methodology and tools and have typically completed four weeks of Six Sigma training. They have demonstrated mastery of the subject matter through the completion of project(s) and testing. Black Belts coach Green Belts and receive coaching and support from Master Black Belts.

The "measure" phase also calls for the data to be plotted to determine the baseline mean, or average, and variation of the sales success for the target group. Variation is quantified by the standard deviation of the data set. Standard deviation is a common metric but widely misunderstood.

To completely understand the concept of standard deviation, the average must be included in the definition. The average of a data set describes the central tendency of the data. Unless each point has the exact same value, the average of the dataset will be different than the value of many of the individual data points. Some values are near the average while others are farther away. The standard deviation can be thought of as the average distance an individual data point is from the average of the entire data set.

Consider the following set of numbers: (8, 8, 12, 12). The average of the numbers is 10; though none of the values actually is 10—they all miss the average. The standard deviation of the set of numbers is the average value by which each of the data points misses the average. In this set of numbers, each of the individual points misses the average by 2. Therefore the average miss is 2. That is the value of the standard deviation.

A high standard deviation indicates wide variation. A low standard deviation represents a very consistent process where most of the data points fall very close to the collective average. Figure 3.3 gives a graphical depiction of this concept.

The average and standard deviation are important benchmarks that establish the starting point, or baseline, of this process. They describe the health of the process at the beginning of the project. They will be used at the end of the project to determine the improvements the project drove. Without these baseline metrics, it would be difficult to know for certain whether the project accomplished anything. All Six Sigma projects require robust measurements.

As described during the "define" phase, the data for this project will the middle 90 percent of the data on sales growth for the first 6 to18 months of a new sales representative's tenure. The project team has collected the data in Table 3.2 from the 60 most recent new-hires.

The graphical distribution in Figure 3.4 shows a few of the data points at the extremes of the distribution.

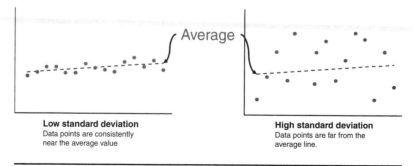

Low standard deviation
Data points are consistently
near the average value

High standard deviation
Data points are far from the
average line.

Figure 3.3 Standard deviation.

Table 3.2 Sales growth—6-18 months.

35.00%	13.60%	10.15%	7.47%
28.00%	13.43%	10.01%	6.76%
22.00%	13.41%	9.85%	6.67%
19.69%	12.46%	9.77%	6.55%
17.55%	12.22%	9.39%	6.49%
17.21%	12.02%	9.15%	5.89%
16.83%	11.86%	9.07%	5.67%
16.57%	11.72%	9.04%	5.51%
15.21%	11.51%	8.82%	5.31%
14.86%	11.15%	8.74%	4.91%
14.74%	10.97%	8.55%	4.11%
14.64%	10.86%	8.37%	3.96%
14.62%	10.73%	8.05%	-4.38%
14.28%	10.62%	7.92%	-7.87%
14.19%	10.29%	7.66%	-14.12%

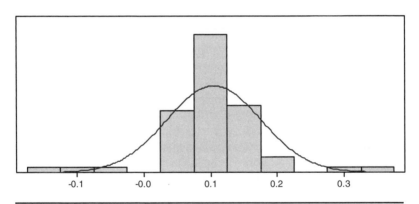

Figure 3.4 New hire sales growth data.

This is raw data that has not eliminated the top and bottom 5 percent of the values yet. As noted in the "define" phase, if the project team believed that some of the extreme performances were solely due the new hire's actions, they could have retained those data points in the final data set. None of the extreme points were kept by this project team. This refinement provides the final data set shown in Table 3.3.

The new graphical summary of the data, Figure 3.5, shows a tighter distribution.

Calculations on the data provide the critical benchmark measures. The average sales growth of the experimental group is 10.6 percent; the standard deviation is 3.7 percent.

Table 3.3   Revised data set.

19.69%	14.62%	11.86%	10.15%	8.74%	6.55%
17.55%	14.28%	11.72%	10.01%	8.55%	6.49%
17.21%	14.19%	11.51%	9.85%	8.37%	5.89%
16.83%	13.60%	11.15%	9.77%	8.05%	5.67%
16.57%	13.43%	10.97%	9.39%	7.92%	5.51%
15.21%	13.41%	10.86%	9.15%	7.66%	5.31%
14.86%	12.46%	10.73%	9.07%	7.47%	4.91%
14.74%	12.22%	10.62%	9.04%	6.76%	4.11%
14.64%	12.02%	10.29%	8.82%	6.67%	3.96%

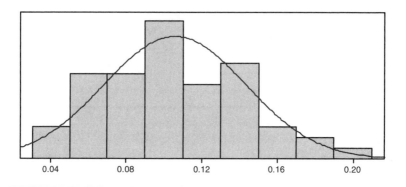

Figure 3.5   Middle 90% of sales growth data.

   With the delivery of a data collection plan, a graphical summary of the data, and the calculation of the benchmark mean and standard deviation, the "measure" phase of the project is complete.

ANALYZE

Thus far, the project team has defined the success metric, collected and graphed the available data, and established baseline values. The Six Sigma roadmap has enabled the project team to provide the data and direction the project needs to move forward with little wasted effort.

   The next challenge for the team is to identify the underlying predictors of sales success. This phase will determine which personality traits prove to be the most significant factors in identifying future sales champions. In order to accomplish this, a list of as many potential success factors as possible needs to be generated. Statistical analysis will evaluate all of these factors to separate the rare "critical few" from the "trivial many" factors that have an actual impact on sales representative success.

Generating this list of possible causes can be accomplished with a couple of brainstorming sessions with the appropriate audiences.

Customers define value, so the customers of this process should be the first ones invited to a brainstorming session. An important question to ask before creating the invitation list is: "Who are the customers of this process?" The intuitive answer would be the external customers that the sales rep calls on, but that conclusion would overlook the intent of this project. The customers of this process are those people who gain value from it. In this case, those people are not the standard "external" customers that the sales rep calls on; the customers of this process are internal.

Since the ultimate goal of this process is to identify predictive factors that will result in higher sales growth, the customers are the sales and marketing leaders who desire this growth. External customers don't really care about the growth rates of their suppliers. They mostly want a good product at a great price. If an external customer were describing his or her impression of a "perfect" sales rep, that customer probably would not give the same description as that rep's sales manager. Some of these potential differences are noted in Table 3.4.

Because of these differences, only internal customers will participate in the brainstorming sessions. Potential participants should include: multiple levels of sales and marketing leadership, sales training, recruiting, and human resources.

In order to have a successful brainstorming session, several common rules should be followed[2, 3]:

- Select a facilitator. This could be the Black Belt on the project. A Black Belt may not add many ideas, since his or her expertise is more focused on Six Sigma and may not be as deep in sales and marketing. However, this lack of bias will aid in facilitation. The facilitator should also record the ideas and act as the timekeeper.

- Avoid criticism. All ideas are welcome. Some of the best may sound silly at first until other people in the room start to build on them with their own ideas.

- Capture all the ideas that are offered on a flip chart or white board.

- Encourage quantity of ideas; quality will come later as ideas are combined and refined.

- After all the ideas are presented, group them into categories. This will provide some overall themes and will facilitate the elimination of redundant ideas.

---

[2] Brainstorming Rules, http://www.isixsigma.com/library/content/t000527.asp

[3] Brainstorming, http://en.wikipedia.org/wiki/Brainstorming

Table 3.4 Customer descriptions of a "good" rep.

Internal customer desires	External customer desires
Price discipline	Price flexibility
Proactive calls	Reactive calls
Hard closer	Gentle closer
Money driven	Relationship driven

Quantity is important, so every possible factor should be considered. Since it is sometimes difficult for the team to start identifying specific factors right away, it may be useful to provide some broad categories. As the conversation gets moving, more categories will emerge. Some useful tools to facilitate this brainstorming session could be fishbone diagrams, mind maps, decision trees, or affinity diagrams. The fishbone diagram in Figure 3.6 lists the possible categories of Work Experience, Life Experience, Education, and Skills.

The factors to be analyzed must be both ethical to evaluate and easy to gather data on. The human resource professional will be expected to ensure that none of the suggested factors violate applicable employment law. Obviously, factors such as race, ethnicity, or gender are illegal and should be ignored. The data this project generates could be potentially sensitive, so it should not be widely distributed.

A potential factor could be a person's level of formal education: trade school, BS, BA, or even a graduate degree. Does a person's college major have an impact on future success? For instance, will a person with a BS in biology be a better pharmaceutical sales rep than one who has a BA in political science? Another popular variable is participation in athletics—organized or otherwise. Athletic participation and achievement is routinely assumed to result in sales prowess. After all, it is not difficult to envision that the same competitive nature that spurs an athlete to win can be transferred from the athletic arena to the boardroom. For athletes, few business endeavors provide the immediate awareness of victory or defeat as does sales. However, this factor may need to be more deeply defined. What if a person possesses a fierce competitive drive but lacks the physical gifts required of a champion athlete; does this factor still apply to them? Does this factor only favor team captains? Does it apply equally to both all-Americans and intramural athletes, or only high school competitors? Statistical analysis can provide answers to these questions. What about previous industry experience? Will the best future copier salesman be one who's been hired away from the competition or will it be an ex-purchasing manager who had to routinely deal with copier salespeople? He may know the sales tricks better than the salespeople do. He may also speak the intended customers' language better than his peers. Does the

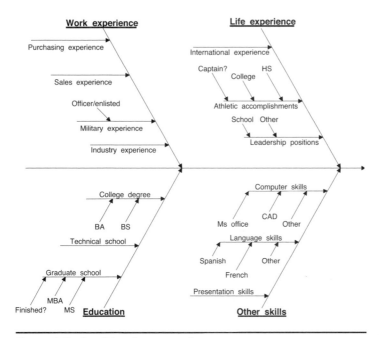

Figure 3.6 Possible sales success factors.

capacity to drive double-digit sales in one industry transfer to another? What about past leadership positions? Did the best future sales representatives hold a student government position in high school or college? Will any leadership position fulfill this requirement? Who will become the better rep, the president of the fraternity house or the president of the honor society? Depending on how the data is analyzed, this project will also be able to rank the factors from most significant to least. It will also answer another important question: "Which factors cannot be linked to sales success?" Veteran sales managers may assume that they already know which factors are most significant. By the end of this phase, the project team will be able to articulate this list with confidence.

Once all of the potential success factors have been identified and agreed upon by the project team, it is time to collect some data. Since success factors are usually consistent over time, data from new-hires as well as veterans can be included in the experiment. The human resource department should already have data on education level, type of degree, college attended, military service, or previous experience. They may have much more. Other data that HR does not have, such as athletic achievements or high school leadership positions, can be collected either with a survey or through the rep's managers.

Before starting any analytics of this project, this may be a good time to explain the concept of how an input variable, such as grade point average, impacts an outcome, such as sales growth. Get ready for a little math, but it will be brief and mostly painless.

There is an important concept in Six Sigma that is written as: "$Y = f(x)$". This is read: "Y is a function of x." The Y represents the *dependent,* or output, variable, which means its value *depends* on the value of some other variable. In this equation, the *independent,* or input, variable is x. A simple example is the algebraic equation "$Y = 2x$". The value of Y is *dependent* of the value of x. If $x = 2$ then $Y = 4$; if $x = 17$, then $Y = 34$. The value of Y only changes if the value of x changes.

In this project, the Y variable represents sales growth. Recall that sales growth in months 6 to 18 is the ultimate measure of success in this project. The aim of this project is to determine which factors positively influence that growth. These factors are represented by the x (independent) variable. So far in this project, some of the x variables that have been identified are: education level, prior experience, athletic participation, and military service. Since sales growth is a function of multiple independent variables, the equation is rewritten as "$Y = f(x_1 + x_2 + x_3 + ... X_n)$; "$n$" is equal to the total number of variables.[4] This relationship between the input and output variables is called the *transfer function.* Now that the concept of the transfer function has been addressed, one other concept needs to be discussed: data types.

Data can be classified many different ways, but the two main categories are *attribute* and *continuous.* Attribute data is simply pass/fail data. Pregnancy is a perfect example of attribute data—a person either is pregnant or is not, there is no halfway. Continuous data is data that can be continuously subdivided, such as time, temperature, or height. Data can often be represented as either attribute or continuous. For instance, temperature can be described as above or below freezing. This is an attribute measure since it can only have two values: "above" or "below" (exactly 32°F will be considered below freezing). Temperature can also be described as a number, such as 33°F. That number, however, can be continuously subdivided: 33.2°F or 33.21°F, or 33.213°F, or 33.2134°F. This ability to continuously subdivide the data is what makes it *continuous* data. Table 3.5 shows how the potential success variables may be measured either as attribute or continuous data.

If given a choice, continuous data is generally preferred over attribute data, since it provides a more accurate description of a metric. Attribute data only provides pass/fail measurement, while continuous data provides information on the relative strength of a data point. Continuous data also provides the opportunity for more complex and accurate analysis. In the temperature example, if measured as an attribute metric, all temperatures below 32°F are treated equally as "freezing." However, as a continuous metric, the large difference between 31.5°F and negative 15.6°F becomes apparent. The cost of the improved accuracy that continuous data provides is that it is generally more difficult to collect. In the temperature example, all that is needed to collect an attribute measure of the

---

[4] x_1 could equal years of athletics, x_2 could equal type of degree, x_3 could equal years of military service, and so on.

Table 3.5 Examples of how the potential success variables may be measured either as attribute or continuous data.

Variable	Attribute measure	Continuous measure
Previous sales success	Forecast achievement?	% forecast achievement
Academic success	College graduate?	Grade point average
International experience	Ever been overseas?	Weeks overseas

outside temperature is a cup of water—if it freezes, it is at or below 32°F. To collect continuous data, a more complex and expensive device (a thermometer) is required.

Multiple statistical tools are available to separate the significant success variables out of the lists generated during the brainstorming sessions. The primary task of most of these tools is to determine whether a perceived difference between two or more data sets is due to coincidence or an actual dissimilarity. For example, if a southpaw kegler made the statement: "left-handed bowlers are better than right-handed bowlers," a right-handed bowler will probably challenge the braggart. To prove his point, the left-handed bowler presents his average bowling score over his last three games, which happens to be two points higher than the righty's lifetime average. The right-hander correctly points out that three games and two points is not enough to support such a broad statement of superiority. The difference could be coincidental. To prove any legitimate claim of dominance, more data is required, but how much—10 games, 50 games, 100 games? How confident is the left-hander in his proclamation of supremacy; would he bet his paycheck on it?

Statistics provides answers to these questions. The primary statistical outcome variable that most Six Sigma professionals use is a figure called the p-value. The technical definition of the p-value is, well, technical. The easier definition is: it is the chance that the difference between data sets is due to coincidence. Therefore, when trying to identify differences, low p-values are good—that is, there is a low chance that a difference is coincidental. p-values range from 0 to +1. A general rule of thumb is that a difference is not *statistically significant* until the p-value is equal to or less than 0.05. That means that there is less than a 5 percent chance that a difference between two data sets is due to coincidence; or, conversely, there is a 95 percent chance that the data sets are actually different. All statistical tests used in this book will be evaluated with p-values.

The decision of which test to use depends on how the data is sorted and the difference to be evaluated. Figure 3.7 lists the various tools that can be used depending on the type of data that is available.

Each test will be explained as it is used in the book.

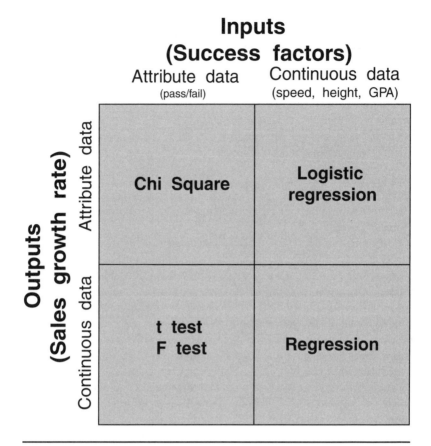

**Inputs
(Success factors)**

Figure 3.7   The various tools that can be used depending on the type of data.

This project could compare sales growth of one group against another, such as those with previous sales experience against those without. Another approach would be to define groups with some specific measure of success, such as having won a certain sales contest or being in the top 10 percent of the population. That would become attribute data (a rep is either successful or not) and all other variables could be compared against that group, or subgroups could be pulled from the entire population (what factor is common to all "successful" reps). Certain, more complex, statistical tests, such as multiple regressions and multivariate analysis, allow more than one variable to be evaluated at once. These tests can identify interactions as well as main effects. A main effect is a single variable, such as whether military service impacts sales growth. Interactions look at two variables; that is, the variable of athletes and military experience alone may not show any significance alone, but athletes who were also in the military may become a successful interaction. Though appropriate for this project, these tests are outside the scope of this book, but a competent Black Belt should be able to perform these analysis. In these examples, only one variable will be evaluated at a time.

Once the data is entered on a spreadsheet, it is easy to adjust the columns and rows to put it into a format that facilitates these comparisons. Ultimately, the data may look something like Table 3.6. Only a few of the data points are represented here; to complete this project data on the success variables would need to be captured for each sales rep in the study.

Don't use gut feeling to determine which factors are important, use some science—guts are never accurately calibrated. Let's say the project team wanted to determine if participation in sports was a significant factor in sales performance. At this point the project team has agreed on the definition of the metric "participating in sports". To start the analysis,[5] segment the growth data between the two groups, as in Tables 3.7 and 3.8.

Table 3.6   Success variables for sales reps.

Sales growth	Athletics	Team captain	Degree	Yrs. sales experience	College leadership
19.69%	y	y	bs	6.5	y
17.55%	y	n	ba	7.2	y
17.21%	y	n	bs	3.6	n
16.83%	n	n	none	8	n/a
16.57%	n	n	ba	6.2	n
15.21%	y	n	ba	4.8	n
14.86%					

Table 3.7   Athletes sales growth.

Athletes sales growth		
19.69%	12.46%	9.39%
17.55%	12.02%	9.15%
17.21%	11.86%	8.74%
15.21%	11.72%	7.92%
14.64%	10.97%	7.47%
14.62%	10.73%	6.76%
14.28%	10.62%	5.67%
13.60%	9.85%	

---

[5] Microsoft Excel is used to perform the statistical analysis in this book. This data analysis capability is available to Microsoft Excel users by simply loading the Analysis Toolpak add-in. Add-ins are found under the "tools" menu. Installation is self-explanatory. Most graphics in this book are originally from Microsoft PowerPoint. A few of the statistical graphics are generated by MINITAB Statistical Software.

Table 3.8   Non-athletes sales growth.

Non-athletes sales growth		
16.83%	10.86%	8.05%
16.57%	10.29%	7.66%
14.86%	10.15%	6.67%
14.74%	10.01%	6.55%
14.19%	9.77%	6.49%
13.43%	9.07%	5.89%
13.41%	9.04%	5.51%
12.22%	8.82%	4.91%
11.51%	8.55%	4.11%
11.15%	8.37%	3.96%

Now it is time for some statistics. The test to determine if the averages of normally distributed[6] data sets are statistically different is the *t*-test or the ANOVA test. The outcome of these tests would determine if the average sales growth is significantly different between athletes and spectators. An ANOVA test provides the following output:

Anova: Single Factor

Summary

Groups	Count	Sum	Average	Variance
Athletes Sales Growth	23	2.721368	0.11832	0.001309
Nonathletes Sales Growth	30	2.936276	0.097876	0.001281

ANOVA

Source of Variation	SS	df	MS	F	P-Value	F crit
Between Groups	0.005442	1	0.005442	4.208154	0.045383	4.030397
Within Groups	0.065948	51	0.001293			
Total	0.07139	52				

---

[6] Normal distribution is the spread of information where the most frequently occurring value is in the middle of the range and other probabilities tail off symmetrically in both directions. Normal distribution is graphically categorized by a bell-shaped curve, or Gaussian distribution. For normally distributed data, the mean, median and mode are very close and may be identical.— www.isixsigm.com

The p-value from the ANOVA output is less than 0.05. As previously discussed, that means that there is less than a 5 percent chance (4.5383 percent in this example) that the difference in the average sales growth between athletes and nonathletes is due to coincidence. In other words, this test indicates with over 95 percent confidence that athletes sell better than nonathletes; therefore participation in athletics appears to be a significant variable in future sales success. The other variables from the brainstorming session can be similarly tested. The lower the p-value, the bigger the difference and the lower chance that the difference is due to chance. Therefore, of all the variables tested, the one that produces the lowest overall p-value is the one that has the largest impact on sales growth (or the one that is least likely due to coincidence). By comparing p-values, the project team will be able to rank the impact of all of the potential factors that were identified.

Statistics can also determine if athletes are more consistent sellers than non-athletes. That is, do athletes sell within a narrow but high band, or are their sales as variable as non-athletes? An F-test determines if there is a statistical difference in the standard deviations of two groups. The F-test returns the following output data:

F-Test Two-Sample for Variances

	Athletes Sales Growth	Nonathletes Sales Growth
Mean	0.118320348	0.097875867
Variance	0.001309289	0.001280828
Observations	23	30
df	22	29
F	1.022220795	
P(F<=f) one-tail	0.470963369	
F Critical one-tail	1.920817283	

In this example, there was no difference in the variation between the two groups. This lack of statistical difference between the standard deviation in sales growth between the two groups is indicated by the high p-value. Since it is above 0.05, the hypothesis that there may be some difference is rejected.

So far, the project team has proven that while participation in athletics seems to positively impact average sales growth, it does not affect the standard deviation versus nonathletes. Other factors could be tested the same way (or even by subgroup factors), such as measuring for success for particular athletes against the whole. For example, it was proven that participation in athletics is a significant variable, but what if only certain athletes, such as swimmers or runners, were compared against the rest of the population? Tests other than the ANOVA or F-test could be used, depending on the data and what is being tested.

Table 3.9   Chi-square analysis of reps by degree.

	Successful reps	Unsuccessful reps
BS degree	4	12
Other degree	7	31

If continuous data is not available, statistics can still identify differences between groups. For example, if the top 20 percent of the experimental group were identified as "successful" and the project team wanted to determine if having a BS degree contributed to their success, another statistical test, the chi-squared test, could be used. The data would be set up as in Table 3.9.

The output of the chi squared test produces a p-value of 0.584, which indicates that the type of degree has no bearing on whether a rep is going to be successful or not. So far, two variables have been evaluated and a link between athletic participation and success has been proven, while no link between degree and success could be established.

Once all the variables have been evaluated, and the vital few important ones have been identified and their level of impact gauged, it is time to use this knowledge to improve the recruiting and hiring process.

IMPROVE

The "analyze" phase of this project verified the factors most significant in forecasting future sales representative performance; equally important, it also eliminated those factors which do not correlate to sales growth. In this example, the project team determined that previous selling experience, athletic participation, and previous leadership roles were all positive factors. Now that these critical success factors have been identified, the sales representative hiring profile can be refined to include them. This awareness of what to look for in a new rep should be shared with internal and external recruiters.

In order to test the new profile, success data on reps hired with the new process system should be compared to those hired previously. Questions that uncover success factors should be incorporated into the interview process. This process may also reveal a need for better consistency during the interview. After all, if all candidates are not interviewed uniformly, then it will be difficult to determine if the new profile is successful. Therefore, recruiters and interviewers need to be trained in how they evaluate candidates. Templates or scripts can be used to help ensure consistency. Once this new recruiting and interviewing method becomes integrated into a company, the templates and scripts will become reference materials to be reviewed as needed.

This is a project that can be continuously improved. Once the initial success profile has been determined, the process could be further refined with additional data, especially sales data of those reps hired under the new model. Continuous analysis of this additional data will provide a more robust and confident structure. This is a very transferable project that can easily be handed over to other business functions.

CONTROL

In order to maintain the benefits this project has uncovered, the findings need to become the default method of evaluating potential new-hires. Whether a company recruits and hires internally or outsources the process, a standardized, fact-based approach needs to become the standard operating procedure. The project team will no longer be responsible for ensuring compliance; they will have handed the new process over to its rightful owners, both sales management and human resources. The new process owners need to be ready to face hiring managers who contest their findings or ask that the criteria be discarded when their gut tells them that they have a winner. Even if the profile is modified for some candidates, simply note how much of the process was followed and why it was discarded. These "discard" data points may ultimately reveal if abandoning the process negatively impacts the hiring process.

This project has defined the profile of a successful sales representative. Now go and hire people who fit the mold.

4

New Product Sales

The lifeblood of most companies is a constant introduction of new products. This is especially true in the medical device, pharmaceutical, electronic, and consumer products markets. For new products to be successful, customers must embrace them early in the launch cycle. This product velocity requirement may sound obvious, but few companies have taken the time to identify the critical factors common to all successful product launches.

Most product launch cycles follow the familiar path of the classic product lifecycle curve, shown in Figure 4.1.[1]

The phases of this curve are generally assumed to change in reaction to the market, and all the collective but uncontrollable forces that shape it. This project takes an internal view of this curve and tries to link the duration of the launch phase of a product to the activities of the sales force charged with selling it.

Even for successful launches, sales of the new product usually increase slowly at first. At this point, only a small segment of the salesforce has actually embraced the product and is actively trying to sell it. The rest of the salesforce is, either consciously or unconsciously, waiting for the market to signal the viability of this new offering. During this phase, most of the salesforce will continue to sell proven products with which they are most familiar. It is easier to sell these well-known products than to commit their resources (time and effort) to an unproven one. Whether the product is ultimately successful or not, few reps are willing to take the lead in selling it because if it fails, the reps do not want to run the risk of their customers blaming them for inferior product. The window for a new product to show its worth to the market is very narrow.

If a product is initially unsuccessful, regardless of the reason, *no* reps will support it and its demise will accelerate until it becomes a market casualty. Companies may attempt to recall the product, improve it, and re-launch, but

---

[1] The Product Life Cycle, www.quickmba.com/marketing/product/lifecycle/

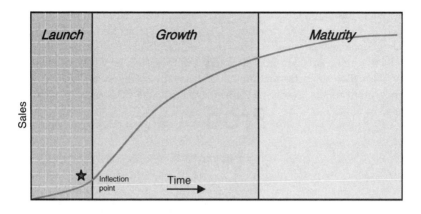

Figure 4.1 Product lifecycle curve.

this is rarely successful since initial impressions (for both reps and customers) are so difficult to change. Product launches usually only provide one shot at success.

Successful products, on the other hand, quickly show their value and begin to gain additional converts in the salesforce. Once a few of the new products have sold, success is signaled and the rest of the salesforce will adopt the product as a reasonable opportunity for success. This adoption will lead to the reps becoming more familiar with the product's features and benefits and more comfortable with the sales process. Concurrently, the market will also become more aware of the product as more customers are introduced to it. The complex synchronization of the supply and demand will raise the sales to an inflection point, at which time the product will enter the growth phase of the lifecycle curve. Sales will quickly accelerate until the product achieves maturity, where sales stabilize.

This same basic path has been repeated for countless products, from countless manufacturers in countless industries, regardless of price or the size of the product launch party. Hoopla surrounding new products is meant to influence how quickly the product will progress through the launch phase and into the growth phase. The secret to a successful launch is to reduce the amount of time needed to reach the inflection point from launch to growth.

Companies try to accelerate this through traditional marketing methods. Internally, companies try to impact this timeline with sales contests and promotions. Sometimes these efforts work and sometimes they fail. It remains to be proven if these promotions and contests influence sales velocity; the prevailing assumption is that they seem to have some effect. Other variables, such as competition and market cycles, also impact adoption rates. Unfortunately, since neither of these factors can be controlled, the project team needs to focus on the variables they can influence. Therefore, they need to identify variables that are both controllable and have the biggest impact on how quickly the product becomes integrated into the market. This project identifies those variables.

DEFINE

"If you can't describe what you are doing as a process, you don't know what you're doing."

W. Edwards Deming

The intent of this project is to decrease time for a product to achieve forecast. To allow for less than perfect forecasting, the project team has elected to revise the project intent to decreasing the time for a product to achieve 90 percent of the sales forecast.

A critical step in the "define" phase of any Six Sigma project is to develop a problem and goal statement that accurately describes the process to be improved and a targeted outcome. More specifically, the problem statement for this project may be written as:

"Based on historical data, it has taken our products an average of 7 months to achieve 90 percent of sales forecast. The goal of this project is to improve this cycle time to less than 5 months. This project should be completed within the next year."

This problem statement follows the *SMART* approach.[2]
It is:

- *Specific* since it calls for a defined outcome.

- *Measurable* since it uses specific metrics to describe both the baseline and the goal. This goal statement also defines a defect in this process; this metric will be used to establish process capability during the measure phase.

The problem statement is also:

- *Attainable*, as the process outcome can be impacted by the company.

---

[2] SMART Goal Setting, http://www.goal-setting-guide.com/smart-goals.html

- *Relevant* to the company since it drives revenue and market share.

- *Time-bound* since it calls for completion within a certain time frame.

The customers of this project are both sales and marketing but will probably be centered in marketing, since marketing is most responsible for establishing (new product) launch strategy. The salesforce is the resource responsible for executing the marketing strategy and customer relationships. Therefore, the project team should have strong representation from both functions. A champion for this project should be able to remove roadblocks in either of these functions: a vice president (VP) of sales and marketing would be a perfect candidate. If this position does not exist, either a VP of sales or a VP of marketing should be able to shepherd this project.

It should also be noted that this project does not examine the complex pre-launch activities a company must complete in order for a product to have a chance at succeeding in the market. This is a very important process, but it is outside of the scope of this project. This project assumes that the product has already completed this pre-launch process and is ready for sale. The present-state, high-level process map in Figure 4.2 captures the critical in-scope process steps.

Veteran marketing professionals will quickly recognize that this process does not contain all of the multiple functions and steps that are required to launch a product. The intent of this process map is to represent this incredibly complex process at its highest level. High-level process maps are very useful problem-solving tools as they define the scope of a project and get everyone to agree on how the actual present-state process looks. This seemingly benign tool can be very powerful since people involved in the project usually assume that everyone views

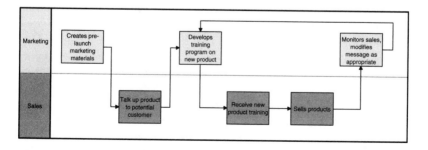

Figure 4.2 Present-state, high-level process map.

the process equally; a high-level process map will quickly uncover divergent views. Lower-level process maps are much more intricate and are not required at this point in the project.

MEASURE

In order to accurately collect process data, a robust data collection strategy needs to be developed. Some of the other projects in this book have called for data that may be difficult to define or collect. That should not be the case with in this project since all companies collect and store sales data. The availability of data, and the probable existence of an established process, should make this project of the more "traditional" projects explored in this book. Since this project lends itself to the traditional DMAIC process so easily, this example will delve deeper than some of the others into the application of specific tools and of their outcomes.

Historical data for this project should be collected from successful launches only. This is an important statement that deserves some explanation. If data from all past product launches were included in this survey, the critical success factors common to successful product launches may be overshadowed by competing factors in unsuccessful launches. Only successful products ultimately pass, and remain above the inflection point, and visit each phase of the product maturity curve. If surpassing this point is a critical measure of success for a project, then these that do not achieve this threshold cannot be included in the calculations.

Depending on the maturity a company, it may or may not have enough product launches to create a robust distribution of fast launch cycle times. However, if multiple products have been launched, the project team can build a frequency distribution of "how quickly a successful product achieves 90 percent of forecast sales." If the project team is dealing with a small number of samples, they may just establish a cycle time average and baseline. Obviously, more data is always better. The project team has been able to collect data from 15 successful product launches; it is summarized in Table 4.1.

Now that the project team has this data, they can perform some basic analytics to provide a statistical description. This will also provide baseline measurements of the process. These metrics will be compared to measurements gathered after the process has been improved to determine the overall project benefit. Figure 4.3 is a graphical representation of the initial data.

The average of the data is 5.89 months and the standard deviation is 1.74 months. Fortunately, the data are also normally distributed. A normal distribution will allow the project team to use common analytical tools and statistical tests to investigate the data. It is also important to look for any obvious trends of groupings, which may suggest the influence of some

Table 4.1 Data from the past 15 successful product launches.

Product	Months to achieve 90% forecast
1	8.6
2	8.4
3	4.5
4	3.1
5	5.7
6	7.0
7	4.9
8	6.1
9	5.8
10	5.3
11	8.5
12	3.9
13	5.0
14	7.3
15	4.2

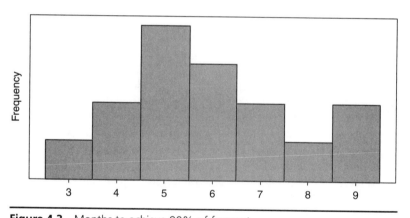

Figure 4.3 Months to achieve 90% of forecast.

unknown variables. In this case, the time-plot of the data in Figure 4.4 does not reveal any.

Figure 4.3 shows most of the data clustered around five months with slightly more data on the right side of the curve than on the left side. There have been a few instances when a product achieved 90 percent of forecast in only three or four months, which is two or three months below the mean it has taken over 8 months 3 times. The project team can use this data to establish the process capability or sigma level.

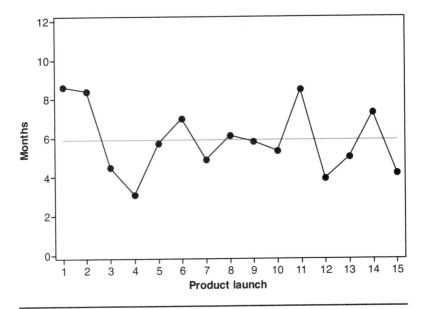

Figure 4.4   Months to achieve 90% forecast.

Process capability describes how consistently a process performs and is described in terms of *sigma levels.*[3] Sigma levels describe the probability of a successful outcome of a process. It is also the basis for the term "Six Sigma." The higher the sigma level, the better a process performs. A six-sigma process fails approximately three times out of 1 million opportunities. A one-sigma process fails about 30 percent of the time. Based on the problem statement, any product that did not hit 90 percent of the sales forecast within five months is considered "defective." The project team wants to reduce the probability of these defects occurring. A baseline sigma measure is calculated to determine the current capability of the process. Some Six Sigma professionals also use the variable C_{pk} to describe process capability. C_{pk} is related to process sigma with the formula: C_{pk} = process sigma ÷ 3.

CALCULATING PROCESS CAPABILITY

There are two ways to determine the sigma level for this process. The first is to calculate process sigma; the second is to use a statistical table called

---

[3] Other terms used to describe process capability include *process sigma* and *Z-score*. These terms can be used interchangeably.

a *Z-table* to determine the process sigma. A *Z-table* is included in the appendix of this book.

The first method of determining the process sigma level is to use the following equation:

$$Z = (USL - \mu)/\sigma$$
Z = Process Sigma, or Z score
USL = Upper specification limit (5 months in our data set)
μ = Process mean (5.89 months in our data set)
σ = Process standard deviation (1.74 months in our data set)

This project is only concerned with defects beyond the upper specification limit. This makes sense since there is no lower specification limit; that is, there is no concern with new products achieving 90 percent of forecast too early. Therefore, the capability of the entire process being successful is equal to the capability of the process to achieve 90% forecast before the 5 months. Finishing the math provides the following output:

$$Z = (5 - 5.89)/1.74$$
$$Z = -0.511$$

This process has produced a negative sigma. This negative score sometimes elicits concern from Green Belts and Black Belts who have heard that "there is no such thing as a negative *Z-score*." This concern is further supported by the fact that there are no negative values (or probabilities for failure over 50 percent) on most single sided *Z-table*.

A negative process capability score does not indicate a miscalculation, although it does signal the presence of a very poor process. Statistically, a negative process capability score simply indicates that the mean of the process is above the upper specification limit. For normally distributed data, this is a sign that more than 50 percent of the process output is considered defective (beyond the specification limit). This is certainly true in this process. Ten of the 15 products listed took over five months to achieve 90 percent of forecast sales, as shown in Figure 4.5.

Since the process mean of this project is above the upper specification limit, and the defect rate is over 50 percent, the process capability score is negative.

Unfortunately, since most Z tables do not contain negative Z-scores, the table cannot be used to determine the probability of a defect.

Fortunately, simple math can fulfill this requirement. Of the 15 data points listed, 10 are defective. Therefore the probability of a defect can be calculated as:

Probability of a defect = $P_{(d)}$ = # defective ÷ # total
$P_{(d)} = 10 \div 15 = 0.667$
Defect rate = 66.7 percent

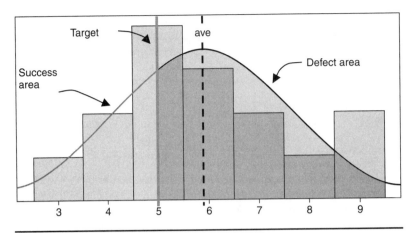

Figure 4.5 Months to achieve 90% forecast.

This represents a 66.7 percent defect rate or, conversely, a success rate of 33.3 percent. Defect rates in Six Sigma projects are often described in defects per million opportunities (DPMO). At a defect rate of 66.7 percent, the DPMO is 667,000.

Between the two methods that have been covered, the baseline process description and capability can be fully described as follows:

Mean	5.89 months
Std Dev.	1.74 months
Z-Score	−0.511
C_{pk}	−0.17
Defect Rate	66.7 percent
DPMO	667,000

The "analyze" phase will determine the root causes of success for the product launch process.

ANALYZE

So far in this project, the issue of poor launch performance has been described first in practical terms and then in statistical terms. The project team has transformed a business problem into a statistical problem. Once the statistical problem is solved, the answer can be converted back into a business solution. Figure 4.6 captures this continuum.

In order to find the statistical solution, and therefore the ultimate business solution, the root causes of variation in target achievement need to be identified and analyzed for their impact on the process outcomes.

The first step in studying to determine root causes is to identify them. The project team should lead brainstorming sessions with business leaders to generate a list of possible root causes.

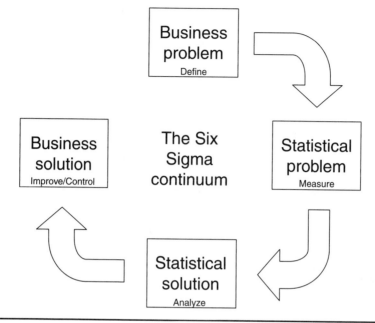

Figure 4.6   The Six Sigma continuum.

A terrific and simple tool to use during these sessions is the cause-and-effect diagram. This is also known as a fishbone or an Ishikawa diagram. These diagrams are often helpful in initiating the flow of ideas started since they provide a framework for organizing the team's ideas. This is done by providing categories for potential root causes. There are several popular categories to use in fishbone diagrams. The "6 Ms" (Measurement, Material, Men & Women, Mother Nature, Methods, and Machines) is one version. Another is the "4 Ps" (Policies, Procedures, People, Plant/Technology). The project team generated the fishbone diagram in Figure 4.7.

When identifying areas for improvement, the project team needs to select variables upon which they can actually have some impact. They obviously cannot control the weather or the competition, so they shouldn't spend time trying to impact those variables. Customers will, ultimately, do whatever they want, despite a sales team's best efforts. An important step in a fishbone exercise is to identify which of the variables is truly controllable and which are not. The factors generated in the fishbone diagram are categorized in Table 4.2.

Another simple tool for determining root cause is the "5 Whys." This tool doesn't require any advances statistics, data segmentation, or even a very

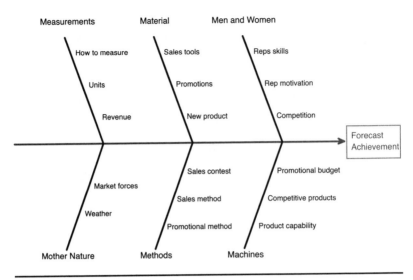

Figure 4.7   Cause-and-effect diagram.

Table 4.2   Categorized factors.

Controllable	Uncontrollable
Reps' skills	Competition
Rep motivation	Competitive products
Sales tools	Weather
Promotions	Market forces
Product capability	
Promotional budget	
How to measure	
Promotional method	
Sales method	
Sales contest	

good data collection plan. It only requires the desire to find the root cause of an issue. This is an especially strong tool when the primary inputs are human factors or when there is not much available data. This is an easy tool to use in almost any problem-solving situation; whether a Six Sigma project or not.

The first step in employing the 5 Whys tool is to have the team agree on exactly what the problem is and how it is measured. This should have been completed in the "define" phase. Second, ask team members what they think is causing the problem. Continue to question the cause of the problem until the team "hits the bottom" and runs out of reasons. The last reason stated should be the root cause of the problem. Asking the question five times is just a rule of thumb. The answer may be determined in fewer then five whys. Asking many more times runs the risk of sounding like a curious four year-old.

In this project, the 5 Whys could be used as follows:

- Why does it take so long for newly launched products to achieve forecast?
  - Because we don't sell enough of them.

- Why don't we sell enough of them?
  - Because not enough of our customers are purchasing the new product.

- Why don't our customers buy enough new products?
  - Because they don't recognize the value of the new products.

- Why don't our customers recognize the value of the new products?
  - Because there has either not been enough advertising or the reps are not focusing on the new products.

- Why has the advertising or rep motivation been weak?
  - Because of the marketing budget or the sales contest budget.

From this simple exercise, a few potential root causes of variation in forecast achievement for new products have been identified:

- Sales rep motivation
- Sales contest budget
- Marketing budget

Each of these factors is partially controllable. These factors were also identified in the fishbone diagram.

All of these elements obviously have some impact on sales. The intent of this phase is to determine which of the three has the *largest* impact. Since we have continuous data (cycle time, budgets, and percentage of salesforce that is selling), simple regression can be used to determine the relationship between the process input and forecast achievement.

Simple regression is a statistical tool that quantifies the strength of a relationship between two variables—a dependent outcome variable and an independent input variable. In our hypothesis, since sales *depend* on the marketing budget, sales becomes the dependent variable. While budget is the independent variable, regression analysis will define the strength of the relationship between the marketing budget and overall sales—that is, does an increased marketing budget result in higher sales? The actual strength of the relationship is communicated via the *r-squared adjusted* value. Simple regression also generates an *r-squared value* (not adjusted). Use the *r-squared adjusted*; it is a more conservative estimate. The technical explanation of the difference between the two is outside of the scope of this book, but it becomes more important when using multiple regression. Multiple regression measures the impact of two or more variables on the process outcome; whereas simple regression only measures the impact of a single variable.

Initially, simple regression will be used to determine the strength of the relationship between the marketing budget and forecast achievement. Later, the marketing budget variable will be replaced with the sales contest budget and, finally, a measure of rep focus. A fitted line plot is a nice graphical output of a simple regression calculation since it provides both the *r-squared adjusted* value as well as a nifty graph that looks great in a PowerPoint presentation. It will also provide an equation of the fitted line through the data. This equation is a useful forecasting tool since it allows users to forecast what a process output would be given a certain set of input variables. Examples of how to do this will be provided as the project data is evaluated. When the *r-squared adjusted* values from the three process hypotheses are compared against each other, they will provide a data-based answer to the question: "What input variable has the most impact on the sales of a new product?" Every function will insist that their input is the primary driver of success. This project will provide a definitive answer.

Table 4.3 is the original set expanded to include the marketing budget for the first year of the product.

Figure 4.8 is the fitted line plot that represents the variable relationship between the marketing budget and months to achieve forecast.

It shows that as the marketing budget increases, the cycle time in months required to achieve 90 percent of forecast generally decreases. Unfortunately, the strength of the relationship, as indicated by an *r-squared* adjusted (*R-Sq(adj)*) value of 36.3 percent, is very weak. A value of at least 50 percent

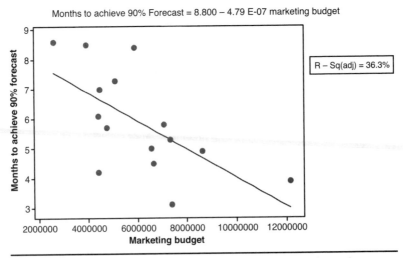

Figure 4.8   Relationship between the marketing budget and months to achieve forecast.

Table 4.3 Data set expanded to include the marketing budget for the first year.

Product	Months to achieve 90% forecast	Marketing budget
1	8.6	$2,592,000
2	8.4	$5,880,533
3	4.5	$6,627,451
4	3.1	$7,359,957
5	5.7	$4,758,041
6	7.0	$4,458,878
7	4.9	$8,622,026
8	6.1	$4,414,365
9	5.8	$7,068,584
10	5.3	$7,309,572
11	8.5	$3,924,492
12	3.9	$12,132,297
13	5.0	$6,537,919
14	7.3	$5,089,077
15	4.2	$4,415,897

would be desired before considering modifying a process.[4] This *R-Sq(adj)* value indicates that only 36.3 percent of the variation in the time it takes to achieve 90 percent of sales forecast is due to the marketing budget. In other words, an increase in the marketing budget was only responsible for 36.3 percent of the total decrease in cycle time. Therefore, some other unknown variable or combination of variables is responsible for the other 63.7 percent. The equation: "Months to Achieve 90 percent Forecast = 8.800 − 4.79 E-07marketing budget" is the equation for the fitted line. It follows the standard equation for a line:

- $y = mx + b$

- y is the outcome (forecast achievement)

- x is the independent variable (marketing budget)

---

[4] In "human-based" processes, *R-Sq(adj)* values greater than 50 percent are worth considering. In a technical process, where more elements can be precisely controlled, *R-Sq(adj)* expectations are much higher (greater then 90 percent).

- *b* is where the line crosses the *y* axis at $x=0$
  - This says that with no marketing budget at all ($x=0$), goal achievement would take 8.8 months.[5] This conclusion sounds a little questionable, and it is. Remember, the confidence of that answer is only 36.3 percent. There is another reason that this conclusion cannot be fully trusted—the math is questionable. Since the marketing budget data does not extend to zero, any estimates made beyond the extremes of the data set cannot be trusted. The regression equation that is produced is only valid within the confines of the data set from which it was calculated. In this case, that range is from $2,592,000 to $12,132,297.

- *m* is the slope of the line. It indicates how much the dependent variable (forecast achievement) changes with each incremental increase in the independent variable (marketing budget).
  - In this example, every additional dollar of marketing budget reduces the forecast achievement cycle time by 4.79 E-07 months, or about 1.24 seconds in a 30-day month.

This finding, no doubt, may disappoint some marketing professionals since they probably assume that the marketing budget would have a larger impact on forecast achievement. The data does not support that assumption. To gain more accurate answers, future tests could focus on specific types of marketing, such as a point of radio versus advertising. This project and the promotion effectiveness project in this book could serve as a guide.

The next step in this project is to use the same method to evaluate the other root cause variables: sales contest budget and rep motivation. If it is assumed that sales contest budgets are actually drivers of rep motivation, then these variables should impact forecast achievement at a similar rate.[6] As long as the data is available, both variables can easily be tested.

The second relationship to be tested is that between sales contest budget and forecast achievement. The launch of a new product is often supported by sales contests. These contests are supposed to inspire the salesforce to sell as much as possible. Depending on the industry, the potential payouts from these contests can be significant. Standard rewards include cash, electronics, stock, or trips. More exotic contests will bestow even more money, longer and more luxurious vacations, and sometimes even expensive motorcycles, sports cars, or powerboats. With so much money being spent on these contests, it is certainly worth determining the impact they have on the success of a product launch. To complete this regression, all the contest prizes need to be measured with a common metric; the most obvious one being the cash equivalent of the prize. This approach could be debated, since a boat as a prize may be more valuable to a rep who enjoys being on the water than to a

---

[5] Months to achieve . . . = $8.8 - 4.79 \text{ E-}07 \times 0 = 8.8$

[6] This concept is referred to as having *covariance*.

landlubber. For this evaluation, however, all prizes are assumed to be equally attractive.

Table 4.4 shows the original data set, expanded to include contest budgets. This is the data that will be used to evaluate the strength of the relationship between months to achieve 90 percent of sales forecast and contest budget.

The outcome of the regression shows that there is, in fact, a fairly strong relationship between the two variables (Figure 4.9). This relationship is much stronger than the one between forecast achievement and marketing budget.

The results show that 60.3 percent of the variation in the time it takes to achieve 90 percent of the forecast appears to be driven by the size of the contest budget. This is an impressive finding since it validates all the money being spent on the sales contests. In fact, by using the formula that the regression produced, the project team can forecast with 60.3 percent accuracy the time it should take to achieve 90 percent of forecast. For instance, if they wanted to know what type of goal achievement $700,000 would drive, they would just substitute that amount for the variable "contest budget."

The project team could calculate the marginal returns of the contest binded.

- Months to achieve 90 percent forecast = 16.53 − 0.000013(700,000)
  - ○ Months to achieve 90 percent forecast = 7.43 months

Table 4.4 The original data set, expanded to include contest budgets.

Product	Months to achieve 90% forecast	Marketing budget	Contest budget
1	8.6	$2,592,000	$671,157
2	8.4	$5,880,533	$743,147
3	4.5	$6,627,451	$724,366
4	3.1	$7,359,957	$915,453
5	5.7	$4,758,041	$766,888
6	7.0	$4,458,878	$781,932
7	4.9	$8,622,026	$881,347
8	6.1	$4,414,365	$731,463
9	5.8	$7,068,584	$901,990
10	5.3	$7,309,572	$835,392
11	8.5	$3,924,492	$633,630
12	3.9	$12,132,297	$928,549
13	5.0	$6,537,919	$892,114
14	7.3	$5,089,077	$641,274
15	4.2	$4,415,897	$894,384

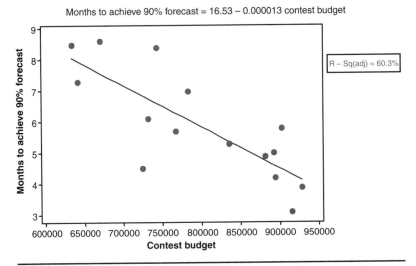

Months to achieve 90% forecast = 16.53 − 0.000013 contest budget

Figure 4.9   Regression showing a fairly strong relationship between the two variables.

- Reviewing the slope of the line
  - For every additional dollar spent on sales contests, the time it takes to achieve the goal is reduced by 0.000013 months
    - 0.000013 months = 33.7 seconds in a 30-day month.
    - So far, this is money better spent than on a marketing budget.

This is a powerful conclusion and the project team may be tempted to wrap up the analytics here, but their work is not quite finished. Recall that they also identified "rep focus" as a potential driver of sales. This may be expected to closely mirror the outcomes of the previous calculation since the intent of sales contests is to encourage rep focus on new product sales. However, if this focus only comes as a result of sales contests, then it comes at a high price. The team needs to determine how to measure rep focus, independent of contest costs.

Since focus cannot be measured empirically, another "proxy metric" that mirrors rep focus needs to be identified. The challenge is to identify a good proxy metric for a variable that is difficult to measure.

The "define" phase of this project identified the project goal as reducing the time needed to enter the growth phase of the product lifecycle. This shift would indicate that this project has managed to accelerate market acceptance of a new product. One of the drivers of market acceptance was identified as the number of reps who were presenting the new product to their customers. Therefore, to achieve product self-sufficiency, it is imperative that a majority of the sales representatives actively sell a new product. With this requirement in mind, the proxy metric for "sale rep focus" will be "percent of sales representatives who have sold the product within the first 6 months of launch."

Additional data has been added to our data-set from the last 15 successful product launches. Each of these new data points represents the percentage of sales representatives that sold the new product within six months of the product launch. This data is attribute data, that is, pass/fail. Under this measurement structure, success is defined as selling at least one product. The actual number of products a particular rep sold does not matter. Therefore, whether a rep sold one unit or 20 units, each is counted equally as a success. If the project team wanted to refine the success criteria, they could subdivide the measurement system into smaller units, that is, selling a minimum number of the new products, or set tiers of success (sold more than 1, sold 1-5, sold 5-10, sold more than 10). Table 4.5 contains the full data set.

The fitted line plot of the data in Figure 4.10 reveals a very strong relationship between the number of reps who sold and goal achievement.

The results show that 83.0 percent of the variation in the time it takes to achieve 90 percent of the forecast appears to be driven by the percentage of reps who sold a new product within the first six months of product launch. According to the regression equation, the time needed to achieve the goal decreased 0.1176 months (3.5 days in a 30-day month) for every additional percentage of the salesforce that were actively selling the product. This finding is especially noteworthy when compared to the impact of the contest budget. These findings may not make sales reps happy, but it is a positive finding for the overall business. The challenge

Table 4.5 The full data set.

Product	Months to achieve 90% forecast	Marketing budget	Contest budget	% who sold
1	8.6	$2,592,000	$671,157	23.5
2	8.4	$5,880,533	$743,147	24.6
3	4.5	$6,627,451	$724,366	43.8
4	3.1	$7,359,957	$915,453	62.0
5	5.7	$4,758,041	$766,888	54.4
6	7.0	$4,458,878	$781,932	33.9
7	4.9	$8,622,026	$881,347	47.5
8	6.1	$4,414,365	$731,463	31.2
9	5.8	$7,068,584	$901,990	35.3
10	5.3	$7,309,572	$835,392	41.5
11	8.5	$3,924,492	$633,630	24.4
12	3.9	$12,132,297	$928,549	61.1
13	5.0	$6,537,919	$892,114	52.2
14	7.3	$5,089,077	$641,274	26.5
15	4.2	$4,415,897	$894,384	53.0

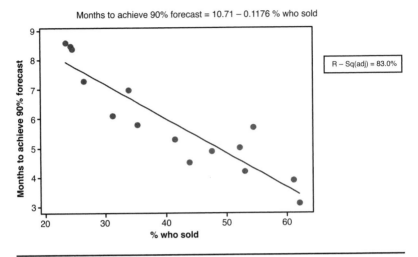

Months to achieve 90% forecast = 10.71 − 0.1176 % who sold

R − Sq(adj) = 83.0%

Figure 4.10   Line plot showing a very strong relationship between the number of reps who sold and goal achievement.

to overcome in the "improve" phase is to develop a process that can motivate reps to sell the product while decreasing the burden of the contest budget.

The three variables that were determined to be most critical in the achievement of the goal of 90 percent sales forecast achievement have now been tested in regard to their actual impact on sales. The results are as follows:

Variable	*R*-squared (adj)
Marketing Budget	36.30%
Contest Budget	60.30%
% of Reps Who Sold	83.00%

The variable that had the greatest impact by far was the percent of reps who sold the product within the first six months.

With the conclusion of these calculations, the project team has prioritized the root cause of forecast achievement and can conclude the "analyze" phase.

IMPROVE

"[Salespeople] are interpreters. But unlike foreign language interpreters, [salespeople] must constantly learn new languages. They must understand the language of each new product, and speak the language of each new target audience."

Jef I. Richards

Now that the data has identified rep focus as the primary driver of success-ful product launches, it is time to validate these project findings by testing them.

The percentage of reps who sold a product in the first six months had the largest impact on the success of a newly launched product. Reps motivation to sell may not be perfectly controllable, but it can certainly be influenced.

In the past, companies have relied on sales contests to encourage sales people to embrace new products and introduce them to their customers. The prevailing wisdom was, to encourage reps to push a new product, management should increase the contest payouts. The assumption that these contests were the most significant contributor to product success was discredited during the "analyze" phase of this project. With this new real-ization, the new question is: "How do we get more reps to sell the product within the first six months?" The answer lies in the new product launch process. The original process was covered earlier, but is shown again in Figure 4.11.

The project findings will not heavily impact the role of marketing in this process, but the pre-launch work of the salesforce will change sig-nificantly. In order to influence and control the number of reps who sell a new product early, sales leadership needs to establish new standards and accountabilities for the sales reps prior to a product launch. Specifically, all reps must identify potential customers in their territories. The first sales calls after the product launch should be customers. The first level of sales management needs to enforce on those accountability to the new process. During one-on-ones or sales reviews, sales managers must en-sure that sales representatives are actively trying to sell the new product to the identified accounts. Marketing should partner with sales to develop a "new product customer profile" that will help sales representatives re-fine their target lists. As additional data becomes available, this profile can be further modified to uncover the best prospects. Additionally, just because this project proved that the percent of reps selling the product is

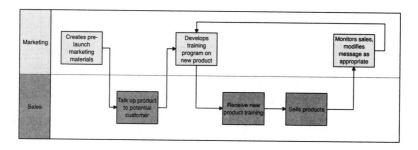

Figure 4.11 The original product launch process map.

a more powerful variable than contest budgets, sales contests should not be abandoned. Contests are still an important part of the sales culture and the simple regression analysis proved that they positively impact sales. Any attempt to eliminate contests could lead to discontent in a salesforce that is accustomed to them. The outcome of this project provides direction on how to spend contest budget more wisely so that they drive the most appropriate behavior. An example of this may be a contest that rewards new product sales to identified, pre-launch customers. Another contest option is to reward the sales team that was able to sell the launch products to the highest percentage of their target customers.

The improved process needs to be documented and disseminated throughout the company, so that all affected functions are aware of their new responsibilities and expectations. The new high-level process map in Figure 4.12 includes a step that calls for the marketing department to create a potential customer profile and for reps to develop target account lists.

To test the new process, the product team needs to collect data on product launches that have followed the "new process." This is where the realities of business may clash with the vision of Six Sigma purists.

Most companies can only manage to launch two to four new products per year. Additionally, only a fraction of these new products are successful. If these challenges were not enough, it is often difficult to determine if a new product is successful for at least 8 to12 months post-launch. At this pace, it may take quite awhile to validate improvements to this process. In fact, if "pure" Six Sigma methodologies were loyally followed and the team demanded a statistically valid sample size to prove the process has reduced the cycle time to achieve the project goal, the "improve" phase of this project could last for years. For those strict Six Sigma professionals, a power and sample size calculation could be run. Less statistically strict (more realistic) Six Sigma practitioners may want to skip the next paragraph.

In calculating the size of a significantly significant sample, requirements were set to show a difference of two months in the average of the sum

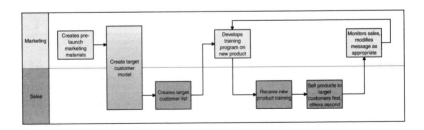

Figure 4.12 The new high-level process map.

of the squares (standard deviation) between data samples. At a power of 90 percent,[7] this would require 17 data points. At three or four launches per year, assuming two of the launches are successful, and recalling that this project only includes those product launches that have achieved 90 percent of forecasted sales, then it would take eight-and-one-half years to collect enough data. In order to see a difference of two months in the mean time it takes to achieve the goal at a 90 percent power level, it would require 11 data points or five-and-one-half years.

Due to these data requirements and the realities of business, the new process should be implemented as the default process as quickly as possible. In the absence of hard, statistical "proof," that show a 1 month improvement from 6 to 5. Any future improvements can be pursued once there have been enough future product launches to build a decent data set.

CONTROL

The new process needs to be incorporated into the business to ensure that the project improvements can be reproduced in the future. Multiple tools can be used to prove that the new process is bearing fruit in the form of improved product launch cycle time. The easiest one to use to look for early indications of a process shift is with a control chart.

Control charts are nice graphical tools that immediately tell a story. They are generally found in the control phase of Six Sigma projects, but can be useful in other phases. They are helpful for identifying whether variation in a process is due to random chance (common cause variation) or due to a specific event (special cause variation). A set of tests called the "Western Electric Company Rules" (WECR) evaluate process variation as common cause or special cause. The WECR are common statistical thresholds and can be found in most statistical software programs either as WECR or "tests for special cause."[7] By using these tests, a process owner can quickly determine if the process has shifted.

The WECR thresholds of identifying variation as special cause require approximately 95 percent confidence. That is, there is only a 5 percent chance that the data pattern is random. This 95 percent confidence is, coincidentally, the same threshold commonly used in most statistical tools, including the ones used in this book (*t*-tests, ANOVAs and *F*-tests). Thus, 95 percent confidence is equal to a *p*-value of 0.05.

---

[7] The "power" of a statistical test is defined as the probability of rejecting the null hypothesis, given that the null hypothesis is indeed false; in other words, stating no difference exists when there is an actual difference. This is also referred to as the Beta risk (β). The difference between this and the p-value, or Alpha risk, is the Alpha risk is defined as the risk of rejecting the Null hypothesis when in fact it is true; in other words, stating a difference exists where actually there is none. Alpha risks relate to confidence intervals and Beta risks relate to power of a statistical test.—http://www.isixsigma.com/dictionary.

Over several years, as additional data from successful product launches is generated, it can be displayed on a control chart. Even if it does not give a perfect answer, it will provide strong directional accuracy about the impact of the process improvements.

The control chart shown in Figure 4.13 is segmented by the "before" process and the "after" process.

The shift in any individual point is not enough to cause the process to violate one of the WECRs, nor are there enough data points to constitute a statistical trend (six points in a row increasing or decreasing), but there is an obvious difference between the two processes.

In the new process, there is a decrease in the mean, but the most significant improvement seems to be in the reduction in variation of the process. The average cycle time for a new product to achieve the target forecast dropped from almost six months to 4.08.

The outcome of the *t*-test shows that the improvement in the average has indeed achieved statistical significance. Remember, though, that these tests will not be quite as valid as would be those with more that data. Unfortunately, more data is not available.

t-Test: Two-Sample Assuming Unequal Variances

	Old Process	New Process
Mean	5.886666667	4.08
Variance	3.029809524	0.107
Observations	15	5
Hypothesized Mean Difference	0	
df	16	
t Stat	3.822511413	
P(T<=t) one-tail	0.000749896	
t Critical one-tail	1.745884219	
P(T<=t) two-tail	0.001499792	
t Critical two-tail	2.119904821	

The *p*-value is less than 0.05; therefore, the null hypothesis is rejected. The null hypothesis was that there is no difference in the averages of the two data sets. In other words, this has proven that the "new" product launch process is, on average, quicker than the "old" process.

The second question the project was to answer is, "Is the 'new' process more consistent than the 'old' process?" The test to determine consistency is the *F*-test, which compares the variance[8] between the two data sets.

---

[8] The terms *variance* and *standard deviation* are often used interchangeably. The relationship between the two measures is that the *standard deviation* of a data set is equal to the square root of the *variance* of the data set.

F-Test Two-Sample for Variances

	Old Process	New Process
Mean	5.886666667	4.08
Variance	3.029809524	0.107
Observations	15	5
df	14	4
F	28.31597686	
P(F<=f) one-tail	0.002684502	
f Critical one-tail	5.873346254	

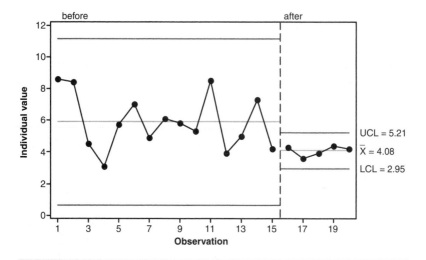

Figure 4.13 I Chart of months to achieve 90% forecast.

The output of the *F*-test also indicates a statistical difference. Therefore, it has been proven that the new process is quicker and more consistent than the old process.

All that is left in this project is to make sure this new method is implemented in all future product launches.

The implementation process for this project can be summarized in two words: *monitoring* and *accountability*. Statistical evidence has proven the impact of changing the standard process, but existing cultural inertia may fight the required cultural change.

Sales reps *must* be required to provide a list of pre-launch target customers. Successful reps and their managers may argue that this project does not apply to them; it only applies to the "other" reps. This attitude could be especially prevalent if the protesting reps have been past champions in new product sales. As a change management technique, it is incumbent that these reps not only are included in this process, but that their efforts and participation be highlighted since other reps will look to them for leadership.

Accountability to the new process by all reps must be driven by the first-level managers and supported by company leadership. They may be uncomfortable in the role of "the enforcer" but they cannot be permitted to shirk this responsibility; it is part of their role as leaders.

Once the reps have identified their pre-launch target customers, they must actually call on these customers and try to sell the new product to them. This should not be construed as not allowing the list of target customers to change. The target customer list can change if new information becomes available that either strengthens the profile of an account that has been omitted, or weakens the profile of a previously included account. If the reps know their customers well enough to accurately select their target customers, these changes should be relatively rare. Any changes must be supported by facts.

When sales managers are discussing sales with their reps, they need to inquire about the sales to the target customers. These sales should be tracked at macro levels at each level of sales management. This data should become a standard agenda item for senior sales staff meetings. If this process is to succeed, it must be tracked, measured, and encouraged. If the new process is not working, sales management needs to understand why.

This project must ultimately be driven by the overall leader of the sales team. One method to encourage the new process is to start every sales meeting or conference call with a review of each sales team's new product target achievement. This focus will drive process adherence.

There are only a limited number of factors that can be controlled in sales. Nothing can be done to control customers or competitors, but companies do have the ability to impact their employees' behavior. This project demonstrates that employee behavior is the most important controllable input variable in the process. Now that this has been revealed, a lack of accountability cannot be permitted to impede the success of this project.

5

Sales Representative Competency

A company's reputation is primarily built upon its products, regardless of what that product or service is. Consequently, companies spend enormous amounts of time, money, and effort ensuring that their products meet some established standard of excellence. These standards can be defined either by the company that produces the product or by the market that consumes them. Some standards, such as safety criteria, are defined by government regulations and are beyond the purview of company leaders.

Product standards change from a confluence of price, cost, customer input, and company reputation. Consistently meeting and sometimes exceeding these standards is a key to success. Consistently good products engender customer trust, so companies work very hard to build that trust. This trust, in turn, facilitates the introduction of future products. As customers become comfortable with one product in a company portfolio, they will be more willing to try future products with less due diligence. This reduced need for sales and marketing outlays results in higher profits.

Every unit a company sells carries its reputation. Even one poor result out of the thousands or millions of units produced could be the difference between delighting a customer and losing them. This balance is further exacerbated by the tendency for unhappy customers to encourage friends to boycott products that have left them unhappy. There is a well-worn business adage that a satisfied customer will tell four or five others about a pleasant brand experience; unsatisfied customers will tell two or three times as many about a poor experience, and up to 50 percent of those potential customers will avoid the tainted company. Additionally, angry customers will continue to boycott companies, and encourage others to do so for decades.[1]

---

[1] Wreden, Nick "How to Recover Lost Customers," http://www.smartbiz.com/article/view/112

Companies are rarely given the opportunity to win unhappy customers back. A study by the Strategic Planning Institute discovered that the average business does not receive complaints from 96 percent of its unhappy customers. At least 90 percent of these noncomplainers will not do business with the company again.[2] This is what rationalizes the efforts that compares funnel into achieving standards and expanding product capabilities. Proof of these efforts is the enormous outlays of money for quality programs, regardless of industry.

The attention given to products is difficult to question, since their success or failure is the lifeblood of a company. But products are not the only profit drivers. *How* a product is sold may be just as important as the product itself. Is nearly as much emphasis placed on the standard of excellence of sales as is placed on products?

Customers perceive sales quality as a reflection of their employer's quality. A rep is not known as just "Mike, the sales rep." He is known as "Mike, the *General Electric* sales rep". By definition, sales representatives *represent* the companies for which they work. Their capability of sales representatives is a perceived reflection of the competency of their company. Great reps inspire confidence in both their employers and their products. Poor reps can inflict damage to a company's reputation that may take years to repair, others may never salvage. Most people can think of an example when a particularly poor sales experience has caused them to permanently boycott a company, regardless of the functionality of the actual product. The sales experience was so unpleasant that it overshadowed the product that was being sold. All the efforts the producer had put into making a great product was damaged due to a bad sales person. Similarly, a pleasant sales experience nurtures confidence in a company and its products. A good rep can make customers forget a lot of product issues.

Competition and dynamic markets demand a constant flow of new products. The demand for competent sales representatives is no less dynamic. Does the company's existing training syllabus address the existing market? As the market and competition have evolved, has sales training evolved to confront this new paradigm?

These questions are not intended to cast doubt on sales representatives' ability to recite the features, advantages, and benefits of their products. Any minimally competent training department should have already enlightened its salesforce about the products they sell. One would further hope most reps could recite the strengths of their products versus the competition. The good reps can probably recite the capabilities of their competitors' products too.

The objective of this project is to define and improve the *other* required knowledge and sales a modern sales representative should process, beyond product awareness. The question this project intends to answer is: "What

---

[2] Lawrence, Kevin. *The 10 Essential Things You Must Know About Your Customers,* http://www.coachkevin.com/page/page/48642.htm

specific skills do sales representatives need to possess in order to sell as effectively and efficiently as possible?"

For this project to work, a company needs to be very specific about what skills it expects sales representatives to have. Just as product managers could easily recite product features they expect sales representatives to know, the company training department should also be able to recite the capabilities it expects its sales representatives to process. These capabilities may not be inherently obvious, so the project team needs to ask three, four, or even five questions deep about these skill sets. "To have strong selling skills" is not nearly a precise enough requirement for this project.

Does the company want sales representatives to possess basic economics knowledge? Should they to be able to read a balance sheet or a schematic diagram? Should the sales representatives possess specific technical knowledge beyond basic product knowledge, such as awareness of basic electrical, mechanical, or chemical concepts? Should the salesforce dress, groom, or speak a certain way? These may seem like trivial questions, but if the recipe for success can be identified, a company will certainly want to repeat it in its most important product, its people.

DEFINE

This project is intended to identify and improve sales representatives' competencies in order to increase sales revenue. Preliminary work will define exactly what these required competencies are. Obviously, the first place to ask is in the sales functions. By surveying the sales leadership, the competencies that are common in the sales champions should become apparent. This project has some similarities to the salesforce hiring profile project covered in chapter 3, but with some important differences. The main differences between a hiring profile and a sales representative competency evaluation is the critical success factors defined by the project. A hiring profile deals with identifying personality traits that are difficult to teach—things like creativity, courage, and ambition. This project is centered on technical skills that can be taught. Hopefully the sales reps being evaluated already possess the appropriate personality traits for success. Once identified and hired, the next step in developing high-value sales professionals is to identify the technical skills required for success and integrate those findings into the sales training curriculum.

Do not limit the identification of sales competencies by surveying only sales leadership. Other functions, such as marketing should also be queried. If financial skills appear to be important, include members of the finance group to identify which specific competencies are the most useful. A company can also identify skills that the market values by trying to identify the skills of their most successful competitors. Like any product on the market, a company's salesforce needs to be at least as competent as its closest competitor.

Finally, the project team should gather voice of the customer (VOC). Customers are the final arbiters of what they consider valuable, since they are the ultimate consumers of the salesforces' competency. Competencies that may seem critical to an internal resource, such as grooming standards may be much less important by customers. Allowing the customer to help define the specifications of the salesforce is no different than asking them to help define the specifications of a new product.

What skills do they expect? The product development group probably already has processes in place to solicit customer input on new products. These processes could be leveraged for this project.

Once all the appropriate individuals and groups have been surveyed, a consolidated list of required competencies should emerge. Hopefully, there will be consistency between what the internal assessors identified and what the customers requested. The competencies can be segmented by affinity group and assigned a weighting by how often a specific skill was identified. That is, skills that were identified by both customers and internal assessors would receive a higher importance weighting than those that were only identified by internal assessors. Table 5.1 lists some possible competencies that customers may raise.

At the end of the "define" phase, the project team should have a complete list of competencies against which to start evaluating their sales force.

MEASURE

The "measure" phase of this project is straightforward. During this phase, the actual competencies of the sales representatives will be assessed against the "ideal competencies" that were identified during the Define phase. These competencies can be assessed either objectively—by testing

Table 5.1 Rep competency list.

Selling skills	Finance skills	Personal skills	Computer skills	Science skills
Completion of selling course in last 24 months	Ability to read a balance sheet	Dress and groom according to company standards	Completion in MS Office Suite user course	Awareness and understanding of basic algebra concepts
Completion of presentation skills course	Awareness of common finance terminology	Emotional quotient awareness training	Completion in CAD program user course	Awareness and understanding of basic electrical concepts
Additional competencies	Additional competencies	Additional competencies	Additional competencies	Additional competencies

Table 5.2 The baseline on sales rep capabilities.

Rep	Sales revenue	Read balance sheet?	Sales skills class?	Presentation skills class?
1	$838,991	1	1	0
2	$1,505,214	1	1	1
3	$898,744	1	1	1
4	$844,539	1	0	0
5	$807,500	1	0	1
6	$1,405,819	1	0	1
7	$1,016,761	1	0	1
8	$1,206,794	1	0	1
9	$1,116,214	0	1	0
10	$603,441	0	1	0
11	$1,031,096	0	1	1
12	$969,631	0	1	1
13	$859,117	0	0	0
14	$754,576	0	0	0
15	$1,093,027	0	0	1

the reps on targeted areas—or subjectively, by interviewing a rep's customers, managers, and peers. For skills such as finance or engineering, a short test that covers critical skills could be administered. Subject matter experts within the company generate test questions. For instance, someone in finance could put together the test questions related to that function. Tests for skills that are new to the company may need to be developed by external resources. For less tangible capabilities such as presentation skills, the evaluation metric would be ratings of the sales representatives by their managers. To ensure that these ratings are effective, use a scale with clear descriptions for each value 1 to 10. Table 5.2 presents the baseline on sales reps capabilities and this current success rate measured by reverse. The table could contain several more columns depending on the industry. Since Excel requires numeric data for statistical analysis, a positive competency is noted by a "one" and a negative competency by a "zero."

There is also a collateral advantage to this project. In order to accurately rate the salesforce, the first-level sales managers will need to actively assess and coach their sales representatives. That is, after all, what they should be doing: providing structured coaching to their reps.

Ultimately, a successful sales project improves the average sales performance of each sales representative and reduces the variation between the top and bottom sellers. If an accurate hiring model for traits and an effective training model for skills can be identified, the result should be a consistently great salesforce.

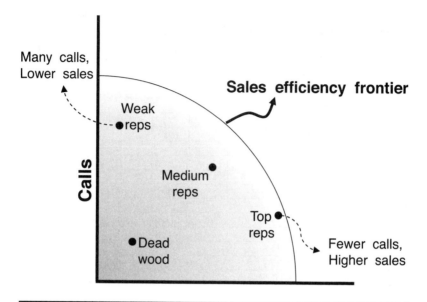

Figure 5.1 Sales efficiency frontier.

The incremental improvement opportunity of each rep is usually correlated to his or her "starting point." That is, top reps are already performing near their potential and do not have as much opportunity to grow as the bottom reps. Figure 5.1 presents the concept of this sales efficiency frontier.

Reps near the outer border of this frontier are performing at the highest efficiency; that is, their sales-to-call ratio is the highest. Those reps, who are already very close to the efficiency frontier, have little room for improvement. Those far from the outer threshold have more room for improvement. Those with the lowest efficiency must either produce significant improvement or should be removed from the salesforce.

The inability for all of the reps to reap equal benefits from this project does not reduce its collective impact. The reps who are performing close to the efficiency frontier are a small percentage of the total population of sales reps, most reps should see improvement.

Figure 5.2 represents the performance of all sales reps for one company.

Imagine that a baseline "defect" limit was set as the bottom 20 percent of sales performers. If the technical skills that facilitate success are identified and applied to the entire salesforce, there would be a broad improvement in sales performance. This impact should be graduated by the individual rep's opportunity for improvement. The low performers on the left side of the curve probably lack the largest number of skills while the highest performers on the right side of the curve have the fewest skill gaps. The majority of the reps, in the middle of the curve, lie somewhere in between the two extremes. Even if the top sellers' performances don't significantly improve but the weaker performers see a large shift to

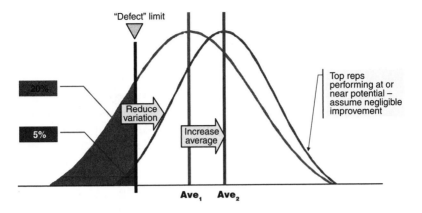

Figure 5.2 Performance of all sales reps.

the right and the middle performers see a medium shift to the right the overall impact is a reduced variation in sales performance and a higher average sales level.

The defect level that originally captured 20 percent of the company has now been significantly reduced. Depending on the original values of the average and standard deviation, the revenue impact of this improvement can be enormous.

ANALYZE

By now, the required competencies of the salesforce have been identified and each of the sales reps has been assessed. Now it is possible to make some decisions from this newly acquired data. During the "analyze" portion of this project the measurement data that was collected in the "measure" phase will be correlated to actual sales performance. Those skills that are proven to provide the most significant impact on sales should ultimately be incorporated in the training curriculum, if they are not already.

The statistical tools used to determine root cause depend on the type of data has been collected, either continuous or discrete. The comparisons will consist of a series of hypothesis tests or regression analysis.

Hypothesis testing is a central concept in Six Sigma and refers to the process of using statistical analysis to determine if observed differences between two or more data sets are due to random chance or to true differences between the groups. For example, if two classrooms were to find the average height of the students in each class, and the average heights were two inches apart, is that difference due to chance or due to an actual difference between the classes? A null hypothesis is a stated assumption that there is no difference in parameters in the datasets (the classes are statistically similar and any difference in average heights are due to chance). The alternate hypothesis is a statement that the observed difference is real and not the result of chance (there is some factor that has caused the average heights to be different—perhaps age, grade, or gender). Hypothesis testing is the process of using statistical tools to analyze data and, ultimately, determine which of the hypothesis (null or alternate) to accept.[3]

Each of the identified competencies can be correlated against sales results to determine which of the many that were identified actually drive sales success. In this example, sales revenue has been identified as the desired outcome of the process. Each of the identified competencies is an input to the sales process. When comparing competencies against one another, the null hypothesis is "none of the competencies has an impact on sales." The competencies that are identified as critical will be the ones that disprove this null hypothesis. As a reference, the chart in Figure 5.3 determines which type of test to use depending on what type of data is being compared.

Since the sales data are continuous, the main tools that will be used are the t-test to compare the means of two data sets and the F-test to compare the standard deviations of the two data sets.

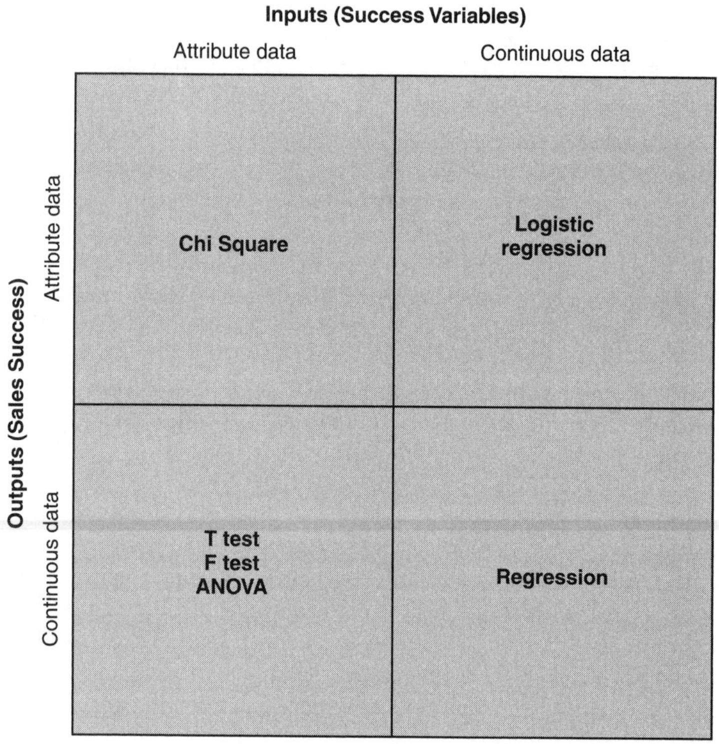

Inputs (Success Variables)

	Attribute data	Continuous data
Attribute data	Chi Square	Logistic regression
Continuous data	T test F test ANOVA	Regression

Outputs (Sales Success)

Figure 5.3 How to determine which type of test to use.

[3] http://www.isixsigma.com/dictionary/Hypothesis_Testing-255.htm

Table 5.2   The baseline on sales rep capabilities.

Rep	Sales revenue	Read balance sheet?	Sales skills class?	Presentation skills class?
1	$838,991	1	1	0
2	$1,505,214	1	1	1
3	$898,744	1	1	1
4	$844,539	1	0	0
5	$807,500	1	0	1
6	$1,405,819	1	0	1
7	$1,016,761	1	0	1
8	$1,206,794	1	0	1
9	$1,116,214	0	1	0
10	$603,441	0	1	0
11	$1,031,096	0	1	1
12	$969,631	0	1	1
13	$859,117	0	0	0
14	$754,576	0	0	0
15	$1,093,027	0	0	1

Revisit the data in Table 5.2

Now that the data is available, the project team can answer the question, *"Does competency in ___ produce statistically higher average sales or variation in sales?"*

The f-test is a generic f-test for a family of 50, including the one-sample *t*, the paired-t, and the two-sided *t*-test. The type of *t*-test that will be used for this analysis is a one-sided, two-sample *t*-test. A one-sided *t*-test provides an indication of "direction" of a higher or lower mean. This test will be used because "direction" is important in this analysis. That is, we are not only interested in whether the mean sales revenues are different by group, but also whether they are different in one direction, in this case, higher. A two-sided *t*-test doesn't differentiate between higher or lower means, only different means. A paired *t*-test links pieces of data together, such as in a "before and after" evaluation. This test could be used to determine the impact of a training program by measuring the performance of sales reps before and after training. The linkage is that it evaluated *same* sales rep. In the calculations being performed for this project, the reps are not linked. It is measuring *different* reps who have been through training.[4] There are two subgroups for the *t*-test as well, one that assumes equal variance and one that assumes unequal variance. If unsure of the equality of the variances, the easiest solution is to perform an *F*-test for equal variances. The *p*-value of this test will tell if the data samples have equal variances ($p \geq 0.05$) or unequal variances ($p < 0.05$). Each of the samples has to be tested individually.

The genesis of the *t*-test is an interesting story that flys in the face of the notion that all statisticians are geeks who don't know how to have fun. The test

---

[4] http://en.wikipedia.org/wiki/Student's_t-test

was developed by a man named William Gosset who worked for the Guinness brewery around the turn of the 20th century. Part of his responsibilities included evaluation of suppliers. It was through his efforts to brew great beer that the *t*-test was developed.[5] This linkage of statistics and beer brewing should not surprise many students of the source, since much of the early study statistics grew out of gambling parlors. There are few other sciences that owe as much of their pool of knowledge to drinking and gambling.

The first factor to be tested is whether the ability to read a balance sheet impacts sales performance. As previously noted, first the two samples will first be tested for equal variance with an *F*-test.

_F_-Test Two-Sample for Variances

	Can Read Balance Sheet	Cannot Read Balance Sheet
Mean	1065545.25	918157.4286
Variance	7.51E + 10	3.58E + 10
Observations	8	7
df	7	6
F	2.101909479	
P(F<=f) one-tail	0.192067157	
F Critical one-tail	4.206668791	

Since the *p*-value is greater than 0.05, the null hypothesis "no difference" is accepted, the variances are not statistically different. The next step is to use a two-sample *t*-test to look for a statistical difference in the means between reps who can read a balance sheet and those who cannot. The output of the test looks like this:

_t_-Test: Two-Sample Assuming Equal Variances

	Can Read Balance Sheet	Cannot Read Balance Sheet
Mean	1065545.25	918157.4286
Variance	7.51E+ 10	3.58E + 10
Observations	8	7
Pooled Variance	5.70E + 10	
Hypothesized Mean Difference	0	
df	13	
t Stat	1.193209676	
P(T<=t) one-tail	0.127054705	
t Critical one-tail	1.770931704	
P(T<=t) two-tail	0.25410941	
t Critical two-tail	2.16036824	

---

[5] http://www.mrs.umn.edu/~sungurea/introstat/history/w98/gosset.html

As previously noted, the single sided, or one-tail, test will be used since the direction of any difference is important in this analysis. Since the *p*-value is above 0.05, there does not appear to be a statistically significant difference in the means of the two data sets, the null hypothesis is accepted.

The other two factors in this example also proved to have equal variance. The outcomes of the *t*-tests comparing the other factors follow. First the *t*-test comparing the performance of those that had completed a sales skill class:

t-Test: Two-Sample Assuming Equal Variances

	Sales Skills Class	No Sales Skills Class
Mean	994761.5714	998516.625
Variance	7.73E+ 10	5.11E+ 10
Observations	7	8
Pooled Variance	6.32E+ 10	
Hypothesized Mean Difference	0	
df	13	
t Stat	−0.028861428	
P(T<=t) one-tail	0.48870674	
t Critical one-tail	1.770931704	
P(T<=t) two-tail	0.977413481	
t Critical two-tail	2.16036824	

There seems to be very little statistical difference between these two groups. This finding is further supported by the fact that their means sales are very similar: $994,761 versus $998,516.

Next is the performance of sales representatives who had completed a presentation skills class:

t-Test: Two-Sample Assuming Equal Variances

	No Presentation Skills Class	Presentation Skills Class
Mean	836146.3333	1103842.889
Variance	2.80E+ 10	52972139200
Observations	6	9
Polled variance	4.34E+10	
Hypothesized Mean Difference	0	
df	13	
t Stat	−2.439326518	
P(T<=t) one-tail	0.014902285	
t Critical one-tail	1.770931704	
P(T<=t) two-tail	0.02980457	
t Critical two-tail	2.16036824	

The *p*-value from this test shows a statistical difference in the average sales performance between groups based on whether they had attended a presentation skills class. Since the single-tailed test was used, this result also shows the direction of the higher mean score. To determine the direction of the superiority, simply look at the means for each of the groups. The group that attended the sales skills class had mean sales of $1,103,842, while the group that had not been through a presentation skills class produced mean sales of $836,146. So the difference in the means is significant and the direction of this difference supports the group that has gone through presentation skills class. Just as these three variables (sales skills, presentation skills, and the ability to read a balance sheet) have been tested, the other potential input variables that the project team uncovered should also be tested.

Some companies may employ more than one salesforce. Pharmaceutical companies often employ several sales groups segmented by product. Each should be evaluated separately to determine if differences are localized to specific groups or symptomatic of the entire company. Another potential variable against which to evaluate sales reps is by manager. This may uncover strengths or weaknesses in the management corps. For instance, a manager in one region may be a more proactive mentor in one or more competencies, while others may spend little time coaching their charges. An ANOVA test could reveal these differences. To test the impact of managers, treat each manager as a separate factor that impacts sales. Other segmentation variables could include time with the company or time in a specific role.

Once the list of vital technical skills has been identified, a second question needs to be asked: "Which skill should be worked on first, and, how long will it take to improve?" Improvement efforts should be prioritized based on the revenue impact they can drive. Other factors to consider include the cost of the training or the ability to even deliver the training. If the competency gap is in a general skill such as finance, potential instructors may be found within the company. If the skill gap is in some other skill for which there is no internal capability, a company may need to look externally for resolution. The use of external resources may increase both the cost of the training and the time to impact.

The list of useful Six Sigma tools that could be used to prioritize teaching opportunities on includes: a prioritization matrix, failure modes and effects analysis (FMEA) or a Pareto chart. Figure 5.4 gives an example of how a prioritization matrix could be used.

In a prioritization matrix, each of the needs criteria is ranked against one another. In this case, low, medium, and high levels of importance have been translated into scores of 3, 6, and 9. This project team determined that the most important consideration was "impact to sales." "Ease of implementation" was rated as medium importance while the "cost of implementation" was rated as the least important, relative to the other factors. The relationship between each option and each needs criteria is also similarly scored. In this example, presentation skills are shown to have a

Needs criteria		Impact to sales	Ease of implementation	Cost of implementation	Total
	Weights	**9**	**6**	**3**	
Options	Presentation Skills	9	9	6	153
	Manager's Skills	6	9	9	135
	Finance Skills	6	6	6	108
	Time in Company	6	3	6	90

Figure 5.4 Competency prioritization.

strong relationship to "impact to sales", so it is scored high, 9. Time in the company was rated as having a weak relationship with "ease of implementation" because experience is so difficult to accelerate. The total scores are calculated by multiplying each option score by its weighting and adding across the rows. For instance, the total for finance skills was calculated as follows:

6×9	(Finance Skills score × Impact to Sales weight)
$+ 6 \times 6$	(Finance Skills score × Ease of Implementation weight)
$\underline{+ 6 \times 3}$	(Finance Skills score × Cost of Implementation weight)
108	

This prioritization matrix has identified presentation skills as the most immediate need of the salesforce, based on the CTQs[6] that were identified, though others could also be added. The second most important success factor was the skill of the manager for whom the rep works.

Now that a prioritized list of critical inputs has been identified, it is time implement the findings in the "improve" phase.

IMPROVE

Gap analysis between actual and target skill levels will identify both the strengths and competency gaps of the salesforce. If a robust and dynamic training department is already in place, then the results should not reveal any significant issues. If sales training has been static and has not evolved with the changing market, large discrepancies may become apparent.

[6] http://www.isixsigma.com/dictionary/Critical_To_Quality_-_CTQ-216.htm: CTQs (Critical to Quality) are the key measurable characteristics of a product or process whose performance standards or specification limits must be met in order to satisfy the customer. They align improvement or design efforts with customer requirements.

Prior to rolling out large-scale training requirements to the entire sales-force, a pilot program should be run to test the proposed solutions. An obvious opportunity to test the suggested improvements would be to pilot different improvements by sales region. This would allow the project team to simultaneously measure the impact of several different training curriculums. Focused training could be provided to reps (and managers) at regional sales meetings. The sales improvement of each of the regions would be tracked and compared against one another. The same hypothesis tests that were used in the "analyze" phase of this project could be used to test the solutions.

Keep the results visible. Outcomes should be graphed against one another to show any diverging trends. This results data should be closely tracked by both the training department and sales leadership and shared with the salesforce. Once the best combination of solutions had been identified, that would become the basis for any permanent changes to the training curriculum.

CONTROL

Completing this project resets the sales training curriculum and creates the training content. During the "improve" phase of this project, the training needed to fill the competency gaps identified during the "analyze" portion was developed. The development and delivery of these training modules should accomplish two things: the first being that the existing salesforce will improve to a standard level of excellence identified in the "define" stage. The second item will be the creation of a training library that reflects the existing challenges of the market. Once this library has been developed, it can be accessed anytime a skill discrepancy is identified.

It should be noted, however, that the development of a training strategy or library was not the ultimate intent of this project. Rather, the intent of this project was to define the critical competencies the salesforce needs to possess in order to increase sales and differentiate themselves from their competition. This subtlety is important to point out since that is the process that should be "locked" during this "control" phase, the process of continuously defining critical competencies, evaluating the salesforce, and responding to the gaps with new training materials.

This process should only change when more effective and efficient ways of executing it are identified; any new competencies must be based on positive sales impact. Figure 5.5 provides the new high-level process map for identifying and training on sales rep competencies.

Both the sales managers and the sales reps should benefit from this project. Sales managers will benefit because they will learn what specific skills and competencies their salesforce need to be successful. This awareness will give them the impetus to do what they should have been doing all along: providing structured coaching and mentoring to their sales representatives. Unfortunately,

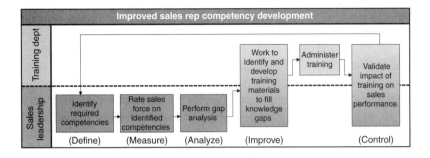

Figure 5.5 Improved sales rep competency development.

this skill is often missing in sales managers. When presenting this project to the salesforce, the project team should ensure that the intent of this project is described as the company taking interest in their capabilities and competencies and investing to improve them.

The amount and type of training a rep receives will depend on that rep's skill level. New sales representatives will, obviously, go through the entire syllabus. Existing sales representatives or managers could receive customized training based on their specific needs.

When training needs have been uncovered and the appropriate curriculum developed, training should be implemented gradually based on the importance of the skill and the gap between existing and target competency. This graduation of training is important to preclude any sudden decline in sales activity. While training is important, the time required to train needs to be balanced against the salesforce's other obligations, especially selling.

The actual training materials should be as dynamic as the market in which a firm competes. The training library will grow as new competencies are uncovered. These may be the result of new products or simply the result of market shifts. Just as computer skills were not critical to a sales representative in 1980, some of the skills that may seem essential today could be obsolete in just a few years. Ultimately, this project should help a company achieve consistent sales excellence in its most important product, its people.

6

The Field-Visit Process

The most fertile interaction between a sales leadership and its field-based employees is the field visit. This is when remote employees have the most significant interaction with one of their company's "leaders." This is also where strengths and weaknesses of individual salespeople are clearly displayed, and can be quickly addressed. When critical information needs to be delivered to the salesforce, the field visit is where the most dynamic commentator take place. The effectiveness of field visits is often a proxy for the effectiveness of sales managers—the field visit is merely one vehicle for them to display leadership. These rep/manager interactions can be the difference between a rep staying with a company or defecting to a competitor; the difference between polishing a promising rep into a superstar and allowing a neutral performer to get stuck in a cycle of mediocre performance. Successful outcomes of these potential recruits can come down to the effectiveness of field visits.

Field visits take place every day but are very poorly controlled. Unfortunately, little VOC has been collected to determine what the customers (sales representatives) of these field visits expect or even the frequency with which they are expected. Few managers make the effort to ask their charges exactly what they expect or want to accomplish on the visits, so the content and agendas are left to their individual whims. This impacts what is, or could be, accomplished.

The current system lacks standardized processes and measures. In most companies, the timing, content, and duration of the field visits is left to the discretion of the sale manager. The worst field visits are the infrequent visits, carried out in near silence by managers who are disinterested or so busy doing "other work" that they barely notices the rep with whom they are riding. Potential field-visit topics of conversation are infinite, but only a few actually provide value. Unfortunately, most field-visit conversations are the polite but noncritical conversations about sports, families, or the weather. These are certainly useful as social lubricant, but should not constitute a majority of the conversation. Value-added conversations are critical business discussions about compensation, selling skills, career, and improving the top line of the company.

In simplest terms, this project tries to answer the questions: "What do field-based employees expect and need from the field visit?" process and "Which field-visit activities and conversations seem to drive the most dynamic performance improvement?" Past investigation by this author into this topic has revealed that the primary areas for focus are the content covered during the field visits and the documentation and follow up before and after a field visit. The goal of this project is to create a standardized, documented, measurable, and repeatable field visit process that meets the needs of both the manager and field rep. The desired outcome of the project is to improve both sales and sales rep retention.

DEFINE

The Define and Measure phases of this project will run almost concurrently because the customers' expectations and current satisfaction level with the process are revealed simultaneously. Since there is usually little baseline data available on the effectiveness of the field-visit process, customers of this process—the field salesforce—need to be surveyed to establish its current effectiveness of the process. The metric that this process is trying to impact is the effectiveness of the current process, gauged both in measurable outcomes, such as retention levels, and in voice of the customer satisfaction scores.

This project meshes closely with the sales representative competency project that was covered previously. Both projects are focused on increasing sales by driving active and structured coaching of the field salesforce by their first level of sales management. Both projects send a tangible message to the salesforce that their management is making an investment to improve their sales skills and their professional growth. This investment should result in a more dedicated, stable, and motivated salesforce. Employees who have confidence in their company perform better and drive greater returns than those who do not.

MEASURE

The Measure phase of this project consists of asking both sales representatives and their managers what they expect during field visits. There are two methods of gathering information: interviews and questionnaires. This is a good opportunity to provide some distinction between the two.

The most effective survey method is personal interviews. These interviews can be delivered either by the company or through an external firm. Personal interviews, especially by outside firms, are expensive, but have the ability to investigate more complex issues than a questionnaire can. Personal interviews can also collect nonverbal data that is lost with questionnaires. Interview requests have higher response rates than other data collection methods and result in fewer incomplete responses or confusion since the questions can be more fully articulated by an external interviewer. Conversely, if the interviewers are company employees, especially sales managers, sales representatives may be reluctant to provide honest evaluations of the existing process for fear that any negative responses may be misconstrued. Another issue to watch for is the impact of recent events. Any event, either positive or negative, will carry additional weight. This can impact both questionnaires and interviews. As with any survey, subjects will probably try to give answers that present themselves in a favorable light.

Surveys can also be self-administered as questionnaires. This method also presents advantages and disadvantages. Questionnaires are far less costly than interviews in terms of both money and time. They do not require a group of dedicated interviewers and can be concurrently sent to a large audience; this is especially true of electronic surveys. The responses from electronic surveys are also available very quickly.

Some of the disadvantages of questionnaire-type surveys included lower response rates and a limited ability to investigate complex issues. They are difficult to complete while a rep is "on the road" since such surveys require them to be sitting in front of the computer. Finally, there is also the concern about the growing number of surveys that the salesforce is already being asked to complete. Any additional requests may be met with skepticism. Regardless of the survey method used, common survey guidelines should be followed:

- Provide preliminary notification of the survey intent.

- Be brief—a single page if possible.

- Maintain focus on the subject.

- Questions should be ordered in such a way that early questions do not influence the response to subsequent questions.

- Do not combine questions with "and" or "or" as the specific response will be difficult to connect back to a specific part of the question.

- Every respondent should be presented with the same questions, in the same order, to eliminate any hidden biases.

- Follow up the survey with a thank-you.

- If possible, assure anonymity.[1]

---

[1] http://www.surveysystem.com/sdesign.htm.

Once the survey data has been collected and consolidated, share it with the group from which it was gathered by all taking a wide-area survey. Pilot or test the survey with a few sales reps and managers and solicit how to improve the survey. Finally, confirm that the survey will be able to collect data. Simple yes and no answers fail to provide magnitude, while text answers provide valuable content. Although the data is more difficult to sort and analyze, sharing the preliminary survey outcomes will foster excitement about the project and get the reps looking forward to the improvements it will drive. Ultimately, the data must be acted upon or the survey will be construed as another useless errand forced onto the sales-force by a disconnected headquarters. Sharing the data will also help drive accountability for completing the project since the sales representatives will be expecting a "new and improved" field-visit process.

Ultimately, the type of survey to use depends on budget, timing, and the type of information being gathered. Factors that impact the survey outcomes include the maturity of the salesforce, maturity of the market, and competition. New reps may be more interested in using the best selling skills while veteran reps may want to focus on career opportunities.

Survey topics and questions can be generated with brainstorming sessions with reps and managers. These sessions should identify areas of miscommunication and opportunities for improvements. If managers think that reps only want to discuss compensation, but the reps want to focus on selling skills, then a critical perception gap is present. During these brainstorming meetings, best practices may also be uncovered. The project team should capture these nuggets since they may become future templates for the improved process.

For an initial benchmarking survey, an electronic questionnaire generally provides adequate data. An example survey will be provided later in the chapter. The survey should cover each aspect of the field visit process.

The field-visit process can be broken down into three major phases: the previsit phase, the intra-visit phase, and the postvisit phase. The data-gathering plan should follow this framework. The previsit questionnaire should uncover items such as how often reps expects a manager to work in the field with them. It should also ask how much advanced notice is desired or what previsit information the reps expect their managers to request. A manager may think that three days' advance notice is appropriate, while a rep may want a week to prepare. The manager could perceive this longer lead time as a delaying tactic to ensure that a day of "home run" calls can be scheduled with safe accounts. Reps, on the other hand, will respond that they want the extra time to ensure that they are getting their managers into the ac-counts where they can make the most significant impact. Setting up these appointments may require more than a few days' notice.

Along with asking what is expected of the process, this project should also document what is actually delivered. Ask reps how many times their manager actually rode with them in the previous quarter or year. How successful was the visit? How is that success measured?

These measurements are going to form the basis for the analysis during the next phase.

To identify best practices, ask the reps what they hope to accomplish during a field visit. Do they want to close some difficult deals or try to foster new relationships? Do they want to exploit their manager's presence, experience, and deal-making authority, or do they want to use their manager as a salve to placate an angry customer? Do they want to discuss career opportunities, compensation, or sales skills? These best practices should also cover the logistics of the field visit: how long do the reps expect these visits to last?

What are managers' expectations of the process? Upon arrival, do they expect a written agenda of the accounts to be visited and issues to be solved? The field visit is the most private meeting that the rep and their manager may get—ever. The time they are together, in between the actual sales calls, is a rare opportunity for them to have each other's undivided attention. What are the current topics of discussion on a field visit? Is the primary topic the collective records of the NFC Central football teams? Is more attention given to a current movie or to sales trends analysis in key accounts? These questions are designed to uncover how much variation exists in the value of the current field visits. This should also uncover the source of this variation. Is the value of field visits dependent on the individual manager? Excessive variation from sales manager to sales manager should be a concern for leadership of a remote salesforce as it indicates excessive variation in the competency of the first level of sales management.

Finally, are there postvisit expectations? Is a follow-up email expected? How quickly should it arrive, and what information should it contain? Field visit documentation is a powerful training and tracking tool. A series of postvisit documents provides a useful narrative of what a rep has (or has not) accomplished during his or her tenure. This documentation also articulates the manager's perception of how well the visits went. It is surprising to see how divergent the opinions of reps and their manager can be when gauging the effectiveness of a field visit. The rep could think that the visits went well while the manager may perceive it as having been a disaster. A postvisit email could help mitigate this confusion. This will also become a useful transitional tool for when managers turn over. Imagine how much more quickly a new manager could "come up to speed" on his or her region if a written history of the predecessor's interactions with reps and customers existed. This would allow the new manager to assess the team's strengths and opportunities much more quickly than if he or she had to learn all of this for themselves. This would also reduce the length of time the reps may feel frustration as they work for a new boss who is unfamiliar with their strengths, weaknesses, goals, and objectives.

A sample survey may look something like this.

Sales Representatives Survey— Field-Visit Process

PRE-FIELD VISIT

1. You receive Pre-field visit notification via:

	Always	Sometimes	Rarely	Never
Letter				
Email				
Voicemail				

2. When you receive previsit letters/notification is there more than 1 week notice?   Yes [   ]   No [   ]

3. The previsit communication (letter/email/voice) sets specific expectations for the field visit.   Yes [   ]   No [   ]

4. Does your previsit communication reference your previous field visit when discussing your development?   Yes [   ]   No [   ]

5. In your opinion, what are the 3 most _____ important items to be covered in the _____ previsit email?   _____

FIELD VISIT

6. How important are each of the following in the field visit?

	Critical	Very	Somewhat Important	Doesn't Matter
DM providing coaching/ feedback				
Career development discussion				
Discussion of Business Plan				
DM time working on territory strategy				
Spending time on my personal development				
DM sharing success stories				
Discussion of competition				
DM providing "bigger picture" to customers				
Product knowledge discussions				

Working on selling skills
DM help selling largest
  customers
Procedural knowledge
  discussions
Role playing

7. Please list any other items you _____
    think would be important to _____
    cover during your field visit. _____

8. How many times did your DM   1× [   ]   4× [   ]
    work with you last year?   2× [   ]   5× [   ]
                                  3× [   ]   5×+[   ]

9. How many field visits per year
    do you expect?   [   ]

10. In the first quarter my
    manager worked with me.   **Yes** [   ]   **No** [   ]

11. How many days did your   1 day [   ]   2.5 days [   ]
    <u>average</u> field visit last?   1.5 days [   ]   3 days [   ]
                              2 days [   ]   longer [   ]

12. How long would do you   1 day [   ]   2.5 days [   ]
    expect the field visits   1.5 days [   ]   3 days [   ]
    to last?   2 days [   ]   longer [   ]

POSTVISIT

13. Did you receive your last field visit
    email within 1 week after
    the field visit?   **Yes** [   ]   **No** [   ]

14. How important are these items in the field visit email?

	Very Critical	Somewhat Important	Important	Doesn't Matter
Action steps to drive sales				
Action steps for development issues				
Development Plan				
Summarization of job competencies				
Working review of Business Plan				
Recap of field visit events				
Recap of YTD sales performance				
Summary of commissions earned to date				
Ranking status in key sales categories				
Commentary drive				

15 Between field visits my manager and I discuss my development progress based upon my last field-visit email.   Yes [   ]   No [   ]

16 Between field visits I have action plans for my development.   Yes [   ]   No [   ]

Since it covers previous field visits and future expectations, the survey output will simultaneously establish both baseline metrics and customer requirements. Both variable and attribute data is being collected, but variable data is more useful since stronger analytical tools can be applied to it. For instance, with variable data it is possible to calculate sigma values for various aspects of the field visit by comparing the survey answers received against a determined "defect." Defect rates could also be established with percentage data. For instance, a defect could be defined as each time a rep does not receive a postvisit email.

The surveys should be completed by both the sales managers and the sales representatives. The example shown is for the sales reps, while a sales manager survey would have similar questions oriented from the sales-manager perspective. Analysis of their answers will provide the data required to identify gaps between the current and target process.

To this point in the project, the team has surveyed the sales managers and sales reps concerning what is expected on a field-visit process. This data has been condensed into a survey to assess the value of the existing field-visit process. The next step in the process is to identify the root causes of strengths or weaknesses.

ANALYZE

During this phase, as in the Analyze phases of other projects the work will be focused on identifying the gaps in the existing process; however, this project also identifies gaps in perceptions between sales managers and reps.

Field-visit standards were determined through the survey process and during the brainstorming session held during the Define phase. For some topics, such as how often a field visit is desired, the gap may be very simple to assess. Gaps in perception on other topics, such as the value of field visits, may be more difficult to assess. The outcome of this survey, however, will identify best practices for future field visits.

Following is a sample of the data from the project team's survey. Each question includes a specification level, outside of which constitutes a defect. This allows the project team to identify the largest issues lie and prioritize their improvement efforts.

FIELD-VISIT SURVEY DATA
Pre-Field Visit Notification

Defect—"Rarely" + "Never"

		Defect Rate
Opportunities	87	36.8%
Defects	32	

Defect—"Less than 1 week notice"

		Defect Rate
Opportunities	35	28.6%
Defects	10	

Field Visit

Defect— "Less than 4 field visits per year"

		Defect Rate
Opportunities	34	38.2%
Defects	13	

Defect— "Less than 2.5 day field visits"

		Defect Rate
Opportunities	36	5.6%
Defects	2	

Post-Field Visit Communication

Defect—"Received later than 1 week after field visit"

		Defect Rate
Opportunities	37	21.6%
Defects	8	

The survey response data allows the project team to develop a prioritized list of improvement plans. The number of field visits per year and previsit communication questions has the highest defect rates in the survey; therefore, that is largest improvement need. With this prioritized list of root cause, the analyze phase is complete.

IMPROVE

The Improve phase of this project consists of implementing best practices or developing new practices to mitigate existing gaps. Over the course of this project, data about how often reps desire field visits, how long they want the visit to last, and what they expect to accomplish during the field visit has been collected. Templates for pre- and postvisit communications can now be created and monitored for effectiveness. The final element required for this project is an implementation plan. In order to do this, the improved process needs to be created and shared. This can take the form of process maps and/or templates for each step in the process. Figure 6.1 is a high-level view of the improved process.

A pilot program can validate the improvements to the process. If the project team has come up with multiple improvement plans, each could be tested in different regions. Once the most successful process is uncovered, it should become the gold standard.

By tracking key performance indicators, trends, both positive and negative, may become apparent more quickly. The most obvious outcome of successful field visits should be a reduction in rep turnover. There are certainly other collateral advantages to this project as well. Happier reps work harder, so if the field-visit process is improved and reps are happier, sales should also increase. A more robust field-visit process should provide more accurate dissemination of information to the field, so calls into sales training, HR, and legal may also decline. More vigilant sales managers with more effective

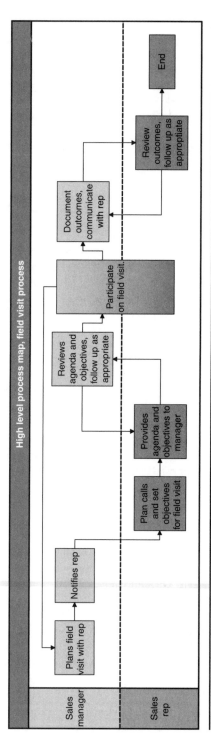

Figure 6.1   High level process map, field visit process.

documentation may be able to identify and terminate problem reps more quickly, which should positively impact customer relationships: Conversely, with all reps being simultaneously evaluated, results should be apparent more quickly.

To determine if the new process delivers its anticipated improvements, the effectiveness of it must be gauged. There are a couple of ways to accomplish this; some are more difficult than others. Linking sales increase to this project may be difficult, since so many other variables also impact sales. However, if all other sales processes remain unchanged and there is an increase in sales, then the project team has pretty firm practical standing that the improvement is due to the project work. Rep turnover, especially new rep turnover, provides a relatively strong link to the health of the field-visit process,[2] so rep churn could be used as a proxy for the success of this program, though this metric is also not perfect. To gain certain validation of the new process, another survey would have to be completed. This should be done only after the new process has been given a chance to stabilize. The follow-up survey could be sent to either a small sample of the original respondents or the entire population. If the appropriate improvements have been implemented, the second survey would reveal this.

CONTROL

In order to ensure that this improved process gets installed as the de facto process, some control plan needs to be created. Implementing accountabilities will ensure that the new process is followed. This is most easily accomplished by disseminating the results of the project with the salesforce. Once the sales representatives know what is expected of their managers, they will help drive compliance by holding their managers to the new standards. Strong messages of support from sales leadership will also bolster adoption of this new process. The new process and expectations that come out of this project also need to be incorporated into the training curriculum for both new reps and new sales managers. Like any good control plan, this one should include provisions of what to do if the process goes "out of control," (that is, the process is not being followed).

Compliance could be accomplished through a hotline or sales-leadership mailbox where reps could voice any concerns. Another option is to make the adherence to this process a constituent of the sales manager's bonus. If some of their compensation is placed at risk, compliance levels should remain high.

This may be a tricky process to keep in place, but if it results in lower turnover, higher sale, more capable sales managers, and more competent sales representatives, then it is certainly worth the effort.

---

[2] This hypothesis could be proven by correlating the turnover rates of high-scoring managers versus low-scoring managers.

7

Sales Territory Planning

Most of the case studies in this book have contained the classic elements of a traditional DMAIC Six Sigma project—that is, they improve an existing process, there is an articulated baseline capability, a defect, and goal. This sales territory planning example is not a traditional "DMAIC project" but rather is an example of that application of Six Sigma tools to evaluate sales territories. This application of Six Sigma identifies which customers to pursue in a sales territory and which to disregard. This "nonproject" is a tangible example of the concept that, even for a Six Sigma company, "everything is not a project." This judicious application of Six Sigma tools, either as a project or otherwise, should be the goal of any company that is trying to adopt the Six Sigma methodology. When Six Sigma is fully integrated into a company's culture, this is how it should be applied—as a set of tools to make fact-based decisions. If every challenge has to be solved as a "project," then Six Sigma will be perceived as an additional level of bureaucracy between business challenges and their successful conclusions, or a method that only Six Sigma professionals employ. In a company that has embraced Six Sigma as the default method of solving business problems, everyone uses a tool to solve all business problems, not just the ones that have been legitimized as "projects." For the sake of consistency, the DMAIC framework has been followed throughout this example.

Now for a quick history lesson about the genesis of an important 6σ tool. In the early 1900s, an Italian mathematician named Vilfredo Pareto was studying wealth distribution in his country. His findings showed that approximately 80 percent of his country's wealth was controlled by about 20 percent of its population. This ratio came to be widely known as "Pareto's Law."[1] In the 1940s, a Romanian-born quality expert named Dr. Joseph

---

[1] http://en.wikipedia.org/wiki/Vilfredo_Pareto.

Juran adapted this principle to his theories about quality. He was the first to describe the concept of "the vital few and the trivial many." It was Dr Juran's theory that 20 percent of the defects in most processes drive 80 percent of the problems.[2] Since this gestation, Pareto's Law, or the 80/20 rule as it is commonly known, seems to have been applied everywhere, including in business. For instance, it is a commonly held belief that 80 percent of a company's profits are driven by 20 percent of its customers.

If this ratio holds true, how many companies manage to this reality? If 20 percent of a company's accounts are so valuable, should they be managed differently than the remaining 80%? For instance, should a company send an inexperienced rep into one of these top 20 percent accounts just because it happens to be in that rep's territory? Should a rep's account list be dictated by geographic convenience or by the nuances of the accounts and the capabilities, knowledge and experience of the rep?

Most sales representative can easily recite the names of their top accounts and approximately how much these accounts purchase. Unfortunately, few reps can provide much additional precision to their descriptions. This lack of knowledge should not be fully blamed on the rep or the manager—it is a responsibility of both understand the inner workings the top accounts. The difference between good and great reps is often just a slight improvements in their depth of knowledge about their accounts. How many managers have partnered with each of their reps to identify what the true profit ratio is in their territories and which accounts actually drive the 50, 75, or 80 percent of the territory revenue? It is this knowledge that will focus on these accounts.

Top accounts are easy to identify and they probably already receive plenty of attention—from everyone. The competition is aware of these accounts too and they are also focusing on selling to them. If a sales rep is being stretched by having to fight stiff competition in these "critical few" top accounts while still covering all the other "trivial many" accounts, then some decisions need to be made concerning the deployment of sales resources. This project mostly focuses on top accounts, but it will also illuminate on the bottom end of the sales spectrum. Just as companies need to recognize the cost of calling on top assets, they need to quantify the cost of calling on the weakest accounts and economize their efforts to ensure that each sales call is driving as much revenue as possible.

If the "trivial many" accounts are not driving appreciable sales or not driving sales commensurate with the effort required to service them, then what is the overall opportunity cost of calling on them? Wouldn't it be more prudent to utilize these efforts and resources toward fighting off the competition at top accounts? Sales representatives only have so many hours per week to call on customers. Companies need to ensure that their

---

[2] http://management.about.com/cs/generalmanagement/a/Pareto081202.htm.

sales reps are applying their limited availability to where the highest payout exists.

An unfortunate but standard response to this business challenge is to ask the reps to "do more"—to make more calls, work longer hours, make more commitments. Ultimately, these increasing requests cannot be sustained. A smarter approach may be to eliminate or reduce the unprofitable activities that are competing for a rep's attention. The largest resource drain a sales force focuses on is calling on the wrong accounts. The realities of a particular market may dictate minor modifications to this approach, but the idea remains the same: reps should spend their valuable time in valuable accounts. The best reps and managers in the company are already doing this—but so are the competition's best reps.

This process may be slightly different across industries depending on how a company sells and what a company sells. Do reps engage in a commodity sale or a consultative sale? Do they compete in a new or mature market? Are they trying to protect market share or grow market share? These questions may alter the project approach, but the core concept of focusing resources on the "right" accounts remain the same.

A concern that may be voiced about a rigorous approach to customer segmentation is captured in the popular adage: "from little acorns grow mighty oaks." It is true that profitable accounts can be cultivated from humble beginnings—after all, every account was small once. This project allows provisions for future high-potential accounts. The process of culling questionable accounts does not mandate abandoning all small customers, but the balance of sales efforts needs to be focused on the most profitable customers, or the ones that possess clear potential to become profitable. There needs to be a sensible business rationale service on an account.

If a rep is calling on a weak account, there needs to be a good reason for this. Reps may call on weak accounts because they are comfortable there, or because they like them, or because the competition is not as fierce. These are all reasons; they are just not *good* reasons. Sales managers need to hold reps accountable for focusing their attention on the most important accounts. How an account is defined as "most important" is determined by a company's sales goals and strategy—it may be sales, growth, potential, or some other metric or combination of metrics. Once that definition is developed, it must become the basis for territory segmentation, and incentive compensation.

DEFINE

Like most territory segmentation efforts, the goal of this project is to improve salesforce effectiveness. But effectiveness, in this case, is not only measured in terms of profit. This project is all about directing sales resources into the accounts that are most critical to achieving sales goals, whether that goal is sales growth, revenue growth, or market share.

Aside from defining the success metric of this project, another requirement of the Define phase is to accurately define who a "customer" is. This seems obvious, but it may not be as simple as it sounds. Is a customer anyone who has *ever* purchased a company's product or service? Is the customer anyone who has shown interest, or is on mailing lists? Does the scope of this project include customers who have purchased products through any distribution method, or is it limited to walk-in customers only? Finally, should there be a time limit on the customer definition? That is, perhaps a customer may be defined as someone who has made a purchase in the last three years. Therefore if someone bought something five years ago but never repurchased, should that individual be counted as a customer? Similar questions can be asked to define what constitutes a sale. The market in which a company competes will help to define these variables.

There are a few ways to gauge the importance of an account. If the primary goal of a company is growth, use growth rates or market share. If a company is trying to maintain market share, use sales revenue or customer churn. Another revealing variable is forecast attainment. Ratio metrics, such as the amount of money that each call generates (*net dollars/call*) could also be used. Utilizing this metric to rate accounts should encourage the deployment of sales resources into the largest accounts, since that is where the highest potential *net dollars/call* ratio exists. If measuring the number of calls is too difficult or burdensome, or inappropriate for a given industry, some other metric may be used, such as *dollars/open house, dollars/trade show*, or *dollars/mailing*. Fortunately, common spreadsheet programs make manipulation and evaluation of numbers very simple. Once a data collection and measurement model has been set up, it is simple to evaluate data sets from nearly any angle. Each will tell a different story and may provide additional insight.

Just as the final variable used to evaluate accounts is up to the project team, so is the data to be used. They could use consolidated data or only use data from certain products or for certain time periods. Whatever measure is ultimately used to compare accounts, the same measure will be used later to drive the new behavior that this project is supposed to encourage.

This project example assumes that profit is the primary goal. Therefore, the most basic sales metric, revenue, will be used. Revenue data will be collected during the Measure phase. Hopefully, historical data exists that will shed light on past distributions of these metrics.

One early finding of this project may be that the revenue generated in the weakest accounts, and therefore their sales call ROI, may actually be negative. This situation will exist if an account's only transactions have been returns of previously purchased products. If this is a consistent pattern, then those accounts should be among the first to go. The company would, obviously, still accept orders, but the sales calls would cease.

MEASURE

"Failure to understand variation is a central problem of management."

Lloyd S. Nelson

An important step in the Measure phase of this project is to review the current distribution of revenue by customer. A basic histogram is a simple but powerful tool that provides a graphical representation of the data. The histogram should be accompanied by the average data of information. This baseline distribution will provide a graphical and numeric summary of the data. Historical sales data identify which accounts drive the most revenue and will also shine a bright light on laggards that drive little or none. Some of these weak accounts may hold promise, but to date they are only consuming resources. Sale rep attention is a resource that may be more effectively directed toward other more strategic accounts.

If there is any question about the accuracy of the sales data that is being delivered, a Gauge R&R[3] study can pin point the source of the inaccuracy. Gauge R&R is outside of the scope of this book, but should not be beyond the capability of a competant Black Belt should be able to complete a gauge R&R study.

Figure 7.1 is a frequency distribution of one year worth of sales data. The graph shows dollars by account. A preliminary gaze indicates that most customers have purchased very little. In fact, the most common revenue figure by account appears to be "zero."

The most obvious characteristics of this data set are its central tendency and variation. These are simple to assess from the graph and provide valuable insight. The accounts are listed from smallest to largest, based on sales. From this preliminary view, it is apparent that the vast majority of customers are not buying much. In fact, most of the customers don't seem to be buying anything at all—the most common data point (mode) is zero. The mean (average) is about $10,000 while the median (middle value) is approximately

---

[3] Gage R&R, which stands for gage repeatability and reproducibility, is a statistical tool that measures the amount of variation in the measurement system arising from the measurement device and the people taking the measurement. This variation is separate from any actual differences between data points (http://www.isixsigma.com/dictionary/Gage_R&R-147.htm). An example would be if an operator needed to measure a part with a caliper, but the operator had not been trained on how to use a caliper. Any variations in measurements from part to part could not be trusted because the measurement *system* could not be trusted.

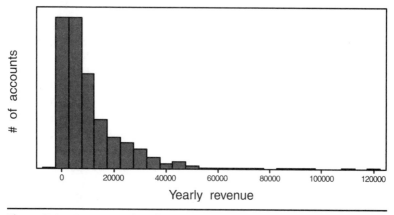

Figure 7.1 Frequency plot of revenue.

$6,500. In normally distributed data, the mean and median are very similar. Their large divergence indicates that the data is scewed to one side. Therefore, the average value, which is usually a very useful metric, reveals very little about the entire data set since a few very large accounts have a large impact on the average. Consequently, the median, which discounts the value of extreme data points, will be used to describe the central tendency. There is also an enormous amount of variation in sales, as described by the standard deviation. The range of sales is from zero (actually just below zero) to over $120,000 per year.

Once this baseline description of the data has been completed, it may be useful to segment the data to reveal other trends and distributions. During the Analyze phase, this data will be examined more deeply to determine the root cause of the distribution.

ANALYZE

The goal of this project is to determine how to best deploy limited sales resources. Basic data analysis will determine where to focus sales efforts. An overall distribution of sales was produced during the Measure phase; the Analyze phase will separate the "good" accounts from the "bad."

One way to accomplish this is with complex spreadsheets, forecast models, and pivot tables. These are certainly useful for "deep-dive" analysis, but it is often much easier to use a simple chart to provide basic direction. A chart tool is also used as a simple tool to deliver information to people who may not be aware of the analytics that have already been completed or are uncomfortable with the cascade of numbers that spreadsheet would deliver. This need to simplify complex data into salient pieces provides an opportunity to introduce the concept of the Pareto chart. As discussed earlier, the Pareto principle contends that 80 percent of a process output is a result of 20 percent of its input.

The Pareto chart is a simple yet powerful tool for displaying data. A traditional Pareto chart lists the contribution of a few main elements to the total throughput of a process. This is analogous to listing the top two or three scorers in a basketball game; they may not have scored all of the points in other words, which 20% of the players that scores 80% of the points, but a small percentage of all the players scored most of the points. A Pareto chart provides a graphical answer the question: "Where are sales coming from?" Does the 80/20 ratio of revenue to accounts hold true, or is it closer to 70/30 or 50/95? A Pareto chart can also be used to highlight the marginal increase in sales as each additional account is considered. As the accounts are segmented by revenue, other questions will arise. An important one to answer is: "What is the cost of servicing weak accounts?" In order to calculate this figure, the project team needs to determine the cost of a sales representative calling on an account. When this cost data is combined with sales data, an ROI figure will become available for each segment of customers.

In this project, the Pareto chart segmentation thresholds may change depending on the distribution of the data being evaluated. The project team may try several segmentation formats until they find the most useful one. In this example, the accounts have been separated by revenue into the top 10 percent, 25 percent, 50 percent, 75 percent, and 100 percent. Figure 7.2 is a Pareto chart of the data. A table that shows the individual and cumulative contribution of each of the segments has also been included.

The first column represents the top 10 percent largest accounts by revenue. Of the 1060 accounts, 10 percent is 106 accounts. These accounts drive nearly 40 percent of the sales revenue and each of those top accounts is worth nearly $40,000. The drop off in profitability from the top 10 percent to the next group (10 to 25 percent) is significant. This chart and table immediately quantify the importance of a very small portion of the entire customer base. This confirmation should initiate the question: "Which reps are calling on these $40,000 accounts? how they are being protected/defended" Accounts that are this attractive to the incumbent vendor will certainly attract the attention of the competition; the competitive activity at these accounts is probably relentless. The current vendor should have its best reps in these top accounts, protecting and growing the business, otherwise it could disappear—the victim of a competitor who secured the account by deploying its finest resources there.

Deeper analysis of account data will provide fact-based suggestions for territory planning. This analysis should also guide the behavior of sales managers. If top accounts are the lifeblood of the company, then both the reps and managers need to be aware of what is going on in them—all the

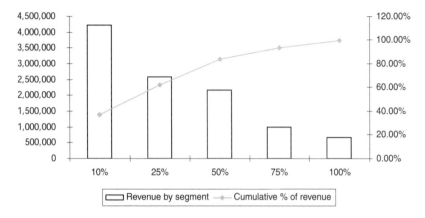

# of accounts	% of accounts	Cumulative revenue	Revenue by segment	Cumulative % of revenue	Marginal revenue by segment
106	10%	4,212,964	4,212,964	39.64%	39,745
265	25%	6,790,671	2,577,707	63.89%	16,212
530	50%	8,957,734	2,167,063	84.28%	8,178
795	75%	9,952,398	994,664	93.64%	3,753
1060	100%	10,627,982	675,584	100.00%	2,549

Figure 7.2   Pareto of revenue.

time. This awareness demands focus and dedication. If a rep is failing to spend the majority of his or her time in top accounts, there needs to be a good reason why—a reason upon which both the rep and the sales manager agree. If the company held a few patents or trade secrets that drove 40 percent of its revenue, you can bet that information would be very well-protected. Are the few accounts that dive the same percentage of business any less important?

In this example, the top 50 percent of the accounts drive 84.2 percent of sales. What percentage of the rep's time is being spent in these accounts? It may not need to be 84 percent of the rep's time, but it should be the majority. Are sales territories segmented to ensure that the largest accounts are receiving the attention they need, both in time and quality of rep?

The sales that these accounts drive is critical, but it may not be the *most* critical factor in territory planning. An equally critical question is, "Which accounts are the biggest drains on our sales efforts, and should therefore be abandoned?"

The bottom 25 percent (1060–795) of accounts drive about 6.4 percent of sales. Any effort that is being expended on these accounts probably will not even produce a positive ROI of the time and effort being spent there. Servicing of an account has a cost. If that cost exceeds the revenue the account produces, then calling on the account is actually producing a negative ROI—that is, calling on the account is a money-*losing* activity. What other money-losing activities does a well-run company voluntarily participate in? Hopefully none. If these accounts are producing negative ROIs, then they should have already seen their last sales rep—unless there is a very good reason to keep calling on them.

Based on this data presented in this graph, *sales reps can reduce their account load by 25 percent and only impact their revenues by 6.4 percent.*

Obviously, this 6.4 percent of lost revenue must be recovered somewhere. It must be recovered in the accounts that are retained. By focusing on fewer accounts, specifically accounts that are driving revenue, the reps should be able to make up the 6.4 percent shortfall. Additionally, the money spent on servicing these bottom accounts can be spent more effectively on producing accounts. Why keep plowing a fallow field?

Leaving even this small amount of revenue "on the table" may seem like an anathema to many sales managers, but this is really a strategic decision and strong strategies require hard decisions. A strong sales strategy is about deploying resources to fit existing and future circumstances, not about servicing single accounts. To focus on single accounts is to lose sight of the ultimate objective—overall revenue growth and market share. These small accounts are not generating much of either and need to be dropped for the overall health of the sales department. In order to make money, a salesforce needs to focus its efforts on where the potential money lies; analysis of the sales data indicates that 6.4 percent of revenues is not worth the resources required.

Figure 7.3 tracks the marginal revenue of each segment of accounts—that is, the average revenue generated by each account in the segment. The data in this chart further support the notion that focusing on the top accounts will drive the greatest rewards.

These data reveal that one account from the top 10 percent of accounts is worth about 16 accounts from the bottom 25 percent. This is calculated by dividing the marginal revenue from a top account by the marginal revenue from a bottom account ($39,745 ÷ $2,549 = 15.59). As previously noted, in order to fully understand if calling on an account is generating positive revenue, a company needs to understand the costs of sending a rep there.

To calculate these costs, the total cost of arriving at the account and spending time there needs to be included in the net revenue calculations. This figure includes transportation, entertainment, and the fixed costs of the sales representative (salary and benefits). Uncaptured, but still very important, is the opportunity cost of a sales rep spending time in a weak account

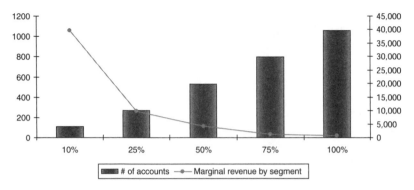

# of accounts	% of accounts	Cumulative revenue	Revenue by segment	Cumulative % of revenue	Marginal revenue by segment
106	10%	4,212,964	4,212,964	39.64%	39,745
265	25%	6,790,671	2,577,707	63.89%	16,212
530	50%	8,957,734	2,167,063	84.28%	8,178
795	75%	9,952,398	994,664	93.64%	3,753
1060	100%	10,627,982	675,584	100.00%	2,549

Figure 7.3 Marginal return by account segment.

instead of spending that time cultivating and strengthening relationships with strong accounts. This cost is further exacerbated by the potentially negative impact of a competitor's rep calling on that "strong" account while the incumbent rep is wasting time in a "weak" account.

Let's say that analysis of historical data has shown that the cost of a sales representative engaging one of these accounts on a sales call is $300. For the sake of this example, assume that the rep calls on the account 12 times per year. Even if the rep is only calling on the weak accounts once per month, a company is still spending $3,600 per year on each of these accounts, *just to show up*. The bottom 25 percent of accounts are only generating, on average, $2,549 per year. A company is losing money every time one of its reps shows up at one of these accounts. Over a year, a company would lose over $1,000 ($3,600 − $2,549) per year, per account. Depending on the number of weak accounts being serviced, this loss could quickly add up. Again, this loss is in addition to the previously mentioned opportunity costs of calling on the "wrong" accounts.

Reps will, unfortunately, sometimes continue to spend time trying to convert bad accounts long after they have proven worthless. This is no surprise, since professional salespeople are inherently optimistic and usually think that they can "turn an account around" if they can just get the customer to understand what a great product they have to offer. An unemotional review of the sales data helps reps make decisions about which accounts to pursue and which to ignore. This is an important advantage of Six Sigma and fact-based decision making—this decision is no longer a personal decision about customers, but a business decision about the account segmentation process.

The decision to ignore customers is a very important one and ultimately depends on many factors. These can include variation in sales from best to worst accounts, the capacity and competency of the salesforce, and the strength of the product pipeline. Ultimately, though, useless customers are going to have to be labeled and discarded.

Analysis of the data has already determined that a top 10 percent account is worth about 16 of the bottom 25 percent accounts. When one considers the time constraints that a modern salesforce is under, this ratio becomes very significant—not only in terms of revenues, but also in terms of employee piece of mind.

If most companies were to survey their reps or employees about their biggest concerns, it would probably learn that people feel saturated with the amount of work that is expected of them. Global competition has forced companies to become leaner. This, in turn, has obligated companies to ask for more productivity out of their employees. The cost of this increased productivity has been an assault on employee's work/life balance. This pressure to produce is probably more tangible to salespeople, since feedback about their work is so instantaneous. By virtue of the sales role, a win or a loss is immediately recognized. Sales representatives have more demands on them then ever before, many of which have very little to do with actual selling. They are asked to develop territory plans, provide competitive intelligence and customer data, and participate in focus groups. They are required to fill out call and expense reports and attend safety, diversity, and product training. They will be asked to sit on steering committees or work teams and fill out surveys for headquarters. Finally, they will be pulled out of the field a couple of times each year to attend regional and national sales meetings. Each of these activities is probably independently useful, but collectively they rob the sales representative of valuable time in front of customers. To make up this customer face time, reps are working longer and doing more administrative work afterhours. This ultimately impacts their job satisfaction and work/life balance. When this balance reaches a tipping point, a rep will leave and the company will be faced with the expense and headaches of an open territory and unsecured accounts.

One way to mitigate this situation is to make sure the reps are spending their time where they can be most successful. It is certainly no secret that it is important to take care of your top customers, but where is the cut-off point between "top," "medium," and "bottom" customers? Unfortunately, conjecture will not provide these limits—once again, analysis result. To determine the limits, run a few data-based scenarios. This analysis will reinforce the worth of the top accounts. It will also quantify the value (or lack thereof) of the bottom ones. A calculation that articulates this difference is the impact of focusing sales efforts in top accounts versus bottom. For instance:

- What would happen if the salesforce just stopped calling on the bottom 25 percent of their accounts?
  ○ In this example, the bottom 25 percent of accounts represents 265 accounts (1,060 − 795 = 265).
  ○ In total, these accounts drive $675,584 in revenue per year.
  ○ This equates to $2,481 per year, per account (657,584 ÷ 265).
  ○ This figure only represents about $200 per account, per month ($2,481 ÷ 12).
  ○ If the bottom 25 percent of the accounts were completely ignored, and all of their revenue was lost, how much would you have to sell in the other accounts to make up for the shortfall?
    ▪ Spread the shortfall over the remaining 795 accounts (1,060 − 265) gives you the following:
    ▪ $675,584 ÷ 795 = $850
    ▪ This says that if the bottom 25 percent of accounts were ignored, the remaining accounts would need to grow by an average of $850.
    ▪ $850, $675,584, represents about 2 percent growth of a top 10 percent accounts, 5 percent of an 11 to 25 percent account and 10 percent of a 26 to 50 percent account.
    ▪ This cost analysis did not account for cost savings generated by not traveling to weak accounts.

This need for an additional $850 per account is an absolute worst-case scenario. This scenario would require *every one* of the bottom 25 percent of the accounts to stop buying *anything*. In reality, the scenario will probably not be nearly as severe since some of the accounts will continue to purchase products, though at a lower rate. If they only bought half as much as they did in the past, the overall shortfall would be only $425 per account.

Another way to evaluate growth that the top accounts drive is to compare how much the bottom accounts would need to grow in order to match modest growth in the top-tier accounts.

- If the revenue of the top 25 percent of accounts grows by 10 percent, how much revenue will that drive?
  ○ $6,790,671 × 110 percent = $7,469,738
    ▪ This represents a growth of $679,067 ($7,469, 738 − $6,790,671).

- In order for the bottom 75 percent of the accounts to equal this revenue, how much must they grow by, on average?
  ○ Sum of bottom 75 percent of accounts = $6,415,018
  ○ $6,425,018 × (Growth rate) = $679,067
    ▪ Growth rate = 11 percent

▪ Think about the impact of this calculation and what it says about the importance of growing top accounts. If the top 25 percent of your accounts grow by only 10 percent, *every one* of the bottom 75 percent would have to exceed that growth rate just to match the revenue. Put another way, the choice is to grow 106 accounts by 10 percent or grow 954 accounts by 11 percent; the revenue impact is the same. Companies need to have a plan in place to grow their top accounts.

The idea that all the accounts in the top 10 percent should be called on consistently by the best sales reps has been well established. These accounts can be referred to as the "A" list. The accounts in the other groups (10 to 25 percent, 25 to 50 percent) should also be called on at a schedule commensurate to their value. The next important task is to develop a plan to identify which accounts to call on that are not on the "A" list, but have to potential to be there. Accounts should not be culled indiscriminately. If there is a good reason to call on a lower-tier account, then call on it. The best reason is "potential."

One way to identify these "sleeping giants" is to identify the common top accounts. If a weak account shares these elements, it may be a "sleeping giant." If sales to hospitals are being evaluated, some of the critical factors may be the number of beds, procedures performed, or patients seen. In financial services, the deciding factor may be length of time a client has been with a firm, total number of services a client uses, or the percentage of a client's net assets that are with the company. In other industries, the deciding factor could be regions of the country, number of employees, delivery trucks or cardboard boxes used. They could even be which competitor is in the account. Regardless of the industry, some factors will be common to all high-potential accounts. If this is the case, then the opportunity to build a profile of what the successful but undersold accounts look like. These are the weak accounts to continue calling on, but with the specific intent of growing them into high-revenue producers.

IMPROVE

The stage has now been set to create a territory plan that matches sales efforts to account value on the appropriate accounts. Historical data and simple analytics have identified where the most potential sales lie. Now it is time to put a plan in place to reap the benefits of this analysis.

If revenue maintenance is the most important sales metric, then reps need to spend most of their time in the accounts that drive the most revenue and ignore the accounts that are not providing an acceptable. Middle accounts should be called on only after the top accounts have been serviced. Promising accounts that are not yet living up to their potential will be given attention commensurate to the revenue they produce. Sleeping giants—low revenue, but very-high-potential accounts—will afford significant attention but with a focus on growth instead of maintenance. If such a policy is implemented, then there will be a plan for every account based on its historical sales and future potential.

Rep focus is the key to the successful implementation of this process. The primary "levers" to modify rep focus are compensation and first-level sales management. Any new compensation plan should recognize the different goals of the various account. Future compensation plans could feature tiered commission structure. Perhaps the top 25 percent of accounts are on the tier 1 accounts. Protecting these accounts is paramount since the loss of one is severe. Compensation on these accounts should focus on protecting market share pay out on the tier 1 accounts should be the highest among all accounts, since these drive the most revenue.

Sales to the second-quartile accounts (25 to 50 percent) will be compensated at a slightly lower level than the top accounts. The incentive compensation model should be aimed at growth. The overall intent is to grow one of these second-tier accounts into a top-tier account. The ones with the highest potential for growth shared identified with the success profile that was created during the Analyze phase of this project. The upside of turning one of theses accounts into a top 10 percent account is huge.

The bottom 50 percent of account should be paid on growth, but at a lower level than the second-quartile accounts. Remember that the intent of an incentive compensation model is to drive appropriate behavior. The highest potential for revenue is in the top accounts. Since bottom accounts should only receive attention after the top accounts have been serviced, the compensation paid to sales in these accounts should reflect this reality. These accounts should receive minimal attention in the absence of extenuating circumstance—circumstances such as new management at the account that may be able to drive growth or a recent merger or acquisition that has improved the revenue opportunities. Otherwise these accounts should receive minimal attention because they drive minimal revenue.

Another important consideration of account segmentation is determining which reps to assign to which accounts. Since "Tier 1" accounts are so strategic, a company needs to ensure that only the best salespeople are calling on them. Such an important revenue source should not be entrusted to a new rep just because it is in his or her territory. This may mandate the creation of a strategic accounts group or creating a hierarchy based on knowledge, skill and experience. Rankings could be: Territory Representative, Territory Manager, and Senior Territory Manager. Perhaps only Senior Territory Managers can call on Tier 1 accounts. These reps have proven their capabilities through subjective and objective evaluations. They are probably career sales representatives who are very familiar with the industry and competition. Their strength is their ability to build relationships with strategic customers. They will manage relatively few accounts, so a collateral duty may include the requirement to mentor novice or less capable sales reps. Their compensation and benefits should reflect their worth.

If a tiered salesforce is adopted, then junior reps will receive compensation and accounts commensurate to their skill level and experience. Only after they have expanded their capabilities—and proven this through subjective and objective display of these new skills—will they begin to reap the level of rewards previously given to senior sales professionals. This segmentation of sales representatives fits well with the Six Sigma project on salesforce competencies that is also contained in this book.

As reps become more capable, they will be entrusted with larger, more strategic accounts, and therefore command increased compensation. This ability to advance should provide the incentive for reps to pursue training or experiences that will expand their capabilities. This demand for improvement will drive sales managers to provide the structured coaching needed to advance these reps. This demand will also drive the sales training department to offer curriculum and programs that will deliver these needed skills. Finally, this tiered sales structure will provide a visible example of a company's dedication to the career path of the long-term, professional sales representative.

CONTROL

If a tiered account management system is adopted, it will be critical to keep the account segments updated. This will probably become an important annual effort. If any "B" level accounts are cultivated into "A" level accounts, the compensation model needs to reflect that change. If any account falls out of its category, an investigation needs to be completed to identify what has predicated the decline; and a recovery plan needs to be implemented.

This project's overall intent is to improve revenue by ensuring that the most important accounts are receiving the most attention. It should also link the most important accounts to the most capable sales professionals, not just the local ones. By abandoning weak accounts, this project should provide the salesforce with some relief from the number of customers they are being asked to carry. It will drive account evaluations away from personal feelings or relationships and toward business realities. Reps should stop feeling obligated to call on friendly but unprofitable accounts and be encouraged to call on profitable accounts, regardless of the customer's personal warmth. The new compensation structure should inspire rookie or marginal reps to improve their skill sets. If customers have questions about a new call pattern, the rep can reference hard data that supports the decision. Territory planning becomes a business decision rather than a relationship decision.

Relationships still drive sales and this project does not intend to change that reality. However, now reps have to make sure they are building and maintaining strategic business relationships with the most profitable accounts— not necessarily the nicest ones.

8

Product Promotion Process

Marketing organizations are responsible for several critical processes, but their primary responsibility is delivering the right information to the right customers at the right time. This is accomplished through the creation and dissemination of marketing materials to existing and potential customers through television, radio, print, the Internet or some combination of the four. The final, and most important, vehicle for dissemenating marketing information is the salesforce. Sales reps distribute marketing information with flyers and brochures as well as with CDs, pens, shirts, hats, flashlights, or whatever other trinkets the marketing group can come up with.

An additional duty of most marketing organizations is the collection and analysis of market and customer data. It is vital that companies have the ability to monitor customer desires and, more importantly, be able to make decisions based upon those desires. Finally, marketing tries to improve sales by creating promotional plans for targeted products.

The number and types of promotions available are limited only by the creativity of marketing professionals. At a high level, they can be grouped into two main categories: customer promotions and rep promotions. These can also be thought of as external and internal promotions. They are differentiated by how the promotional benefit is assigned: to the customer or to the rep. The type of promotion used for a particular situation depends on several variables, including but not limited to: the type of product being promoted, the maturity of the product, competition, customer needs, and the intended outcome of the promotion.

An external, or customer, promotion is intended to increase sales by providing the customer with a real or perceived incentive to purchase a product or purchase additional quantities of a product. These promotions are useful for selling commodities that have several substitutes in the market. Any advantage, price or otherwise, that the promotion provides over competing substitutes should spur additional sales. Promotions that offer price concessions, extra quantities, or prizes do not require much additional sales rep effort, so these promotions can be cycled rapidly or left in place for long periods of time.

Internal, or rep, promotions direct the promotional benefit of the sale to the rep by providing some tangible reward or incentive. Rep promotions, by virtue of their definition, do not provide any incentive to the customer. Rep promotions are best used for items that require consultative sales skills. The sales of these items are usually influenced by the application of additional sales resources—namely, sales rep effort. It should be recognized, however, that since a rep's effort is a finite resource, rep promotions approximate a zero-sum game. If additional effort is expended on selling the target product, then less effort is available to sell all the other products, so the number of products, promoted and non-promoted alike, sold could remain roughly constant. The impact that promotions have on revenue depends on the margin of the promoted product as well as the ones that are disregarded in its favor.

Internal and external promotions can be further subdivided. For the purposes of this review, each type will be subdivided into two additional categories. Customer promotions will be covered first. This promotion type will be subdivided into a "price discount" category and a "free product" category.

A price discount promotion, as the name implies, encourages additional purchases by reducing the price of a product. These are the ever-popular "10 percent off"-type of promotions. Sometimes, price promotions are accompanied by coupons or rebates that customers must redeem in order to receive the concession. Price discounts are, by far, the most common type of promotion.

Free-product promotions also encourage additional purchases, but the promotion payout is made in additional product. These take the form of "buy four get the fifth one free"-type promotions. A price promotion and a free-product promotion may actually achieve the exact same monetary discount for a customer.[1] A promotion that advertises "buy four get the fifth one free" provides the exact same benefit as a "20 percent off" promotion—as long as the customer needs five of whatever product is for sale.

The effectiveness of a promotion lies in the customer's perception of the benefit. If a customer perceives one type of promotion as being more valuable, whether math supports this perception or not, then the promotion has accomplished its purpose.

A free-product promotion has the potential to raise sales in the short term but may hurt long-term sales as customers build additional inventory in order to qualify for the discount. Other types of promotions are not as vulnerable to this lingering effect, but neither are they immune.

Customer promotions do not provide any benefit to the sales representative; in fact, if a rep is paid on margin, customer promotions could actually be a disincentive for them if the price reduction impacts their compensation.

Rep promotions can also take on multiple forms. This study will evaluate two types: the "spiff" promotion and the "prize" promotion. A spiff, also

---

[1] This discount may be different for the product manufacturer, due the spread between sales price and production costs.

know as "push money," is a small monetary bonus or additional commission that is paid out to sales reps for selling a particular product. This may take the form of a promotion that pays a sales rep $50 for every one of the targeted products they sell. Additionally, spiff promotions can be applied to entire sales teams—"All the reps in the Eastern region will receive a $250 bonus if they can collectively sell 500 widgets by the end of the month."

Prize promotions encourage reps to sell targeted products by giving the reps the opportunity to a prize to win some type of prize. Reps are made eligible for a prize drawing, or receive additional chances to win, then based on sales of the targeted products. Obviously, the ultimate prizes and the perceived chances to win, then impact the success of this type of promotion. Rewards often include luxury trips, expensive prizes, or cash bonuses.

Rep promotions do not direct any of the benefit to the customers who purchase the products, but they direct the salesforce's attention toward these customers. Figure 8.1 shows the different promotion types.

Sometimes customer and rep promotions are run concurrently. This may ultimately increase sales, but the root cause of the sales increase or the relative impact of each type of promotion cannot be determined since there are multiple competing drivers of the increase. This project utilizes Six Sigma tools to determine which type of promotions are the most effective at increasing sales.

DEFINE

The goal of this project is twofold. First, the project intends to show if promotions have any effect on the sales of a targeted product. The second and more important goal is to determine which of the four types of promotion is the most effective at increasing sales.

A successful promotion is defined by its intent. A successful promotion can be defined as one that lifts the sales of a targeted product, either by a targeted amount or just above the pre–promotional sales levels. A defective

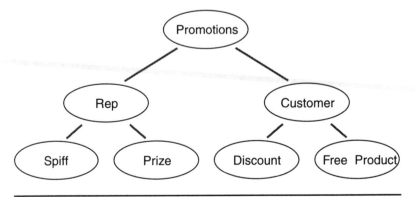

Figure 8.1 Promotion types.

promotion would fail to do so. As previously stated, this project attempts to identify which type of promotion drives the largest lift in sales of the promoted product. This is not the only measure that can be used. Success can be also defined as identifying the type of promotion that produces the most rapid increase in sales, the most consistent increase in sales, or the most sustained increase.

As with any DMAIC project, a high-level process map should be completed prior to entering the "measure" phase. Figure 8.2 is a SIPOC of the sales promotion process.

MEASURE

During the "measure" phase, a data collection strategy should be developed and deployed. If available, historical data should be collected to establish the baseline impact of past promotions. Each previous promotion should be categorized as an internal spiff, internal contest, external discount, or external free product. If none of these types of promotions have been used, this project can be easily modified to evaluate alternate promotions. It is up to the discretion of the project team to include data from other sales activities, such as coupons, point of sale, or rebate promotions.

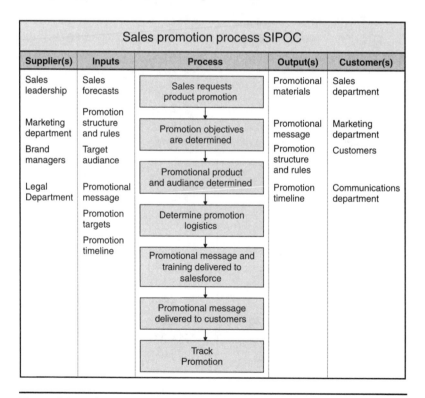

Figure 8.2   Sales promotion process SIPOC.

Accurate data that links sales to a specific promotion may be tough to acquire due to the difficulty in correlating sales to a specific promotion. This task is further aggravated due to the ubiquity of promotions in many industries. If multiple promotions are being run concurrently, it is difficult to determine the impact of any single one of them. It may also be difficult to determine what the "no promotion" sales level is. This is important data to capture, however, since it provides the "starting point" against which the effectiveness of future promotions will be evaluated. If this is the case, one technique to alleviate this issue of multiple concurrent promotions is to eliminate all promotions for long enough for the market to reach its steady state. This plan to cease all promotions may meet with significant consternation, especially if promotions are standard in the industry or if they are perceived to be a powerful factor in generating sales. Table 8.1 captures the baseline (no promotion) sales in four regions.

Fortunately for this project team, they were able to store all promotions.

Table 8.1 Prepromotion sales results.

Western	Northern	Eastern	Southern
$9,876	$15,452	$15,122	$12,480
$14,855	$19,197	$11,383	$6,425
$15,890	$9,611	$11,486	$7,555
$10,494	$21,327	$11,599	$9,872
$12,501	$20,037	$14,633	$10,882
$10,817	$17,368	$14,441	$13,612
$11,798	$10,397	$13,845	$11,084
$16,056	$10,538	$12,364	$13,957
$12,024	$25,130	$16,490	$9,527
$14,324	$7,197	$10,738	$8,546
$9,658	$14,067	$16,158	$15,058
$12,521	$14,441	$13,163	$7,779
$15,592	$10,029	$12,816	$9,364
$10,931	$21,735	$15,672	$10,230
$12,607	$15,545	$15,266	$7,104
$17,876	$22,372	$14,302	$11,588
$11,644	$20,679	$14,786	$11,974
$16,317	$18,631	$12,361	$5,772
$14,667	$12,741	$13,088	$13,690
$16,179	$6,233	$12,657	$12,774
$14,519	$24,234	$14,234	$10,921
$16,927	$11,821	$12,915	$11,939
$16,269	$13,329	$11,172	$7,197
$17,919	$19,439	$11,242	$10,140
$17,072	$25,503	$13,323	$5,065

Stopping all promotions may be a difficult step to implement, but it is the most accurate way of determining the effect of a specific promotion. Fortunately, this requirement to achieve the "no-promotion" baseline may be avoided.

If the same promotions are running concurrently in all territories, this "multipromotion environment" could be considered the steady state, since no single territory is being shielded from variables to which other territories are being exposed—they are all equal. This is analogous to a basketball game in which the players wear hiking boots. If all the players wear the boots, no single player gains an unfair advantage. The negative variable of wearing hiking boots is being equally applied to everyone. Therefore, if one player outscores the others, the difference cannot be attributed to the defenders wearing hiking boots, since the offense wore them too. Some other variable must be responsible for that player's success. This concept can be applied to promotional sales. If every territory already has multiple, but equal, promotions being run, the positive impact of each of the promotions is equally shared among the territories.

If this approach is taken, then the "multipromotion" balance must be preserved throughout the course of the project. If this balance is upset, it will be difficult to identify the root cause of any change in sales. It could be the result of either the experimental promotion or the termination or modification of an existing promotion.

Another important factor to consider when evaluating the impact of promotions is the effect of seasonal sales fluctuations. If sales move in a predictable cycle, then that cycle should be accounted for when evaluating the effectiveness of promotions. Otherwise, a seasonal uptick or decline may be incorrectly attributed to the promotion. These fluctuations are relatively simple to identify with past sales data plotted year versus year, as in Figure 8.3.

This chart shows a consistent decline in sales in April, June, and October. March is routinely the most lucrative month. Any promotions would need to account for the cycle. The best way to eliminate the variable of seasonal fluctuations is to run the experimental promotions concurrently.

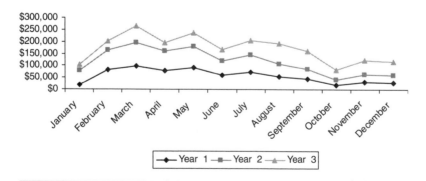

Figure 8.3   Southern region sales.

Once all external variables have been accounted for in the design of the promotion experiment, multiple controlled promotions can be introduced throughout the country and the sales data can be collected. Which of the four promotions is run in any particular territory should be randomized. This can be achieved by using the random number generator or by just drawing names out of a hat. This randomization will further protect the experiment from any lurking but unidentified variables.

Running multiple different promotions concurrently throughout the country looks benign on paper, but it has the potential to spark dissention in the participants. Recall that much of the value of a promotion is in the perception of the individual who receives an advantage from it. This difference in perceived value applies to both customers and sales reps. Sales reps who are not participating in an internal spiff promotion may feel slighted by those who are. The nonparticipating reps may believe that they are missing an opportunity for increased compensation. On the other hand, the reps who are missing out on the opportunity to offer discounts to customers may feel that their sales (and thus their compensation) are being compromised for the sake of a headquarters experiment. Customers, if they become aware of the experiment, may voice similar concerns. Even if the ultimate discount is equal between a price discount promotion and a free-product promotion, someone will perceive one as being more valuable than the other. If this issue is not handled quickly and professionally, it could result in a lost or disappointed customer or sales representative. A project team should be ready for these potential issues. Overcommunication prior to any differentiated promotions will help mitigate any issues. These potential pitfalls illustrate why being able to collect past data based on historical promotions would make this project easier.

In order to evaluate the different promotions, the project team has to make a few assumptions. They should assume that the capabilities of each of the sales representatives participating in the promotions are equal. They should also assume that the market demand for the target products is equal in each of the areas where the promotion has been or will be run. Finally, the project team should assume that competition is equal in each of the sales areas.

Even if some variation exists within each of these variables (reps, territories, competition), if territory segmentation and sales training is applied consistently throughout the entire sales region, and the market is not abnormally controlled, then in aggregate the ultimate impact of each of these variables should balance. The same can be said of competition. If this is not the case and the market, competition, or even customers are significantly different in certain territories, then data from these territories should not be included in the project. If this questionable data is included during the "analyze" phase, it may create false signals that could lead to inappropriate modifications to the process during the "improve" phase.

Some sales professionals will resist these assumptions. They will honestly believe that their territories, sales representatives, or competitive threats are inherently different from those of their peers. Each will be able to provide multiple reasons why they deserve special consideration. If any of these perceptions can be proven with data, then some of the project assumptions can be adjusted. If these concerns cannot be proven and supported with data, then they should be discarded as myths. If these assumptions are not made, the number of impact variables quickly grows to a point that will make completing the analysis nearly impossible.

Whether the data was gathered through the collection of historical data or from launching multiple experimental promotions, it is available in Table 8.2.

Table 8.2 Sales promotion results.

Western	Northern	Eastern	Southern
Spiff	**Contest**	**5 for 4**	**20% discount**
$11,587	$16,271	$16,645	$13,770
$15,402	$20,107	$13,387	$6,758
$16,259	$10,707	$13,189	$8,580
$10,692	$23,831	$12,483	$11,091
$14,405	$23,249	$15,536	$11,640
$11,846	$19,266	$16,098	$15,614
$13,491	$10,655	$14,270	$11,862
$16,339	$11,682	$13,100	$14,797
$12,724	$26,028	$16,594	$10,708
$16,171	$7,650	$12,240	$9,389
$10,472	$15,905	$16,591	$15,381
$13,667	$16,892	$13,261	$8,323
$16,768	$10,639	$14,223	$9,918
$11,947	$22,694	$15,712	$11,468
$14,284	$15,869	$16,701	$8,077
$19,532	$23,141	$14,865	$13,303
$11,655	$21,361	$15,221	$12,709
$18,278	$20,849	$13,100	$6,713
$15,950	$13,897	$14,511	$15,622
$18,197	$6,307	$14,473	$14,204
$16,187	$24,895	$15,704	$12,529
$17,163	$11,981	$12,984	$13,123
$17,040	$13,791	$12,951	$7,236
$18,121	$19,995	$13,079	$10,691
$18,224	$26,583	$15,311	$5,128

As with any data set, the first step is to plot the data and develop a statistical description. Figures 8.4, 8.5, 8.6, and 8.7 are graphical displays of each of the promotion data sets. Statistically, each data set is normally distributed.

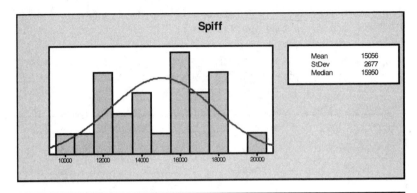

Figure 8.4 Promotion data set: spiff.

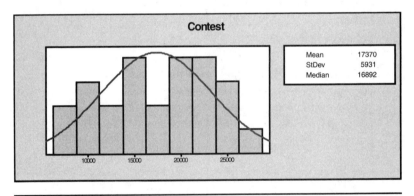

Figure 8.5 Promotion data set: contest.

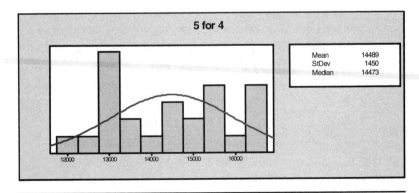

Figure 8.6 Promotion data set: 5 for 4.

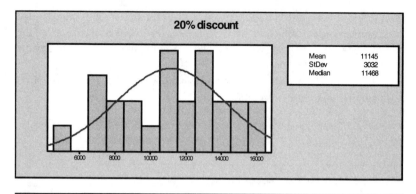

Figure 8.7 Promotion data set: 20% discount.

With this step, the "measure" phase is completed. So far, the project metrics have been identified, and a data collection plan has been conceived and executed. Historical data has been collected and process variation has been determined. The process performance baselines have been calculated. It is now time to identify which of these promotions is the most successful at improving sales.

ANALYZE

During the "analyze" portion, the project team will calculate the impact of the various types of promotions on sales. Sales data has been collected on each of the promotion types. Now those data sets can be evaluated against each other to determine if there is a difference in the sales impact of the different promotions.

There are two null hypotheses that this project will test. The first is "promotions do not have any impact on average sales." The second null hypothesis is "there is no difference in average sales between promotions." The project team will employ a *t*-test and an ANOVA test to accept or reject these null hypotheses.

The first null hypothesis to be tested is "promotions do not have any impact on average sales." To determine the validity of this statement, the project team will compare data points from 100 sales territories both before and after a promotion. At this point, no differentiation is being made between the types of promotion. The only metric that matters is whether there was a promotion or not; this is pass/fail data.

As previously mentioned in this book, the appropriate statistical tool to use to compare the averages of two continuous data sets is the *t*-test. A *p*-value of less than 0.05 indicates that there is a significant difference in the average sales level during a promotion. A p-value greater than 0.05 will indicate that the promotion has no effect on the average sales level. Since "direction" of the improvement is important (we expect the promotional sales to be higher), a one-tailed t-test will be used.

This is the Excel output of the t-test that compared average promotion sales against average nonpromotion sales:

t-Test: Paired Two Sample for Means

	Promotion Sales	Pre Promotion Sales
Mean	14515.12	13461.77
Variance	18003038.58	16629019.02
Observations	100	100
Pearson Correlation	0.9881	
Hypothesized Mean Differnce	0	
df	99	
t Stat	15.8716	
P(T<=t) one-tail	2.94552E-129	
t Critical one-tail	1.6604	
P(T<=t) two-tail	5.89104E-29	
t Critical two-tail	1.9842169	

The p-value is less then 0.05, therefore, there is a statistical difference in the means between the two groups. Additionally, the mean is higher for the promotional sales group.

Since the outcome of the first t-test has proven that there is a statistical improvement in average sales during a promotion, the second null hypothesis can be tested. If this second round of analytics determines that there is a difference in sales depending on the promotion type, then the project team will finish its analytics by determining which promotion is the most effective.

To answer the second null hypothesis question, an ANOVA test will be used. The t-test was used initially since the means of only two groups were being compared (the promotion and the no-promotion groups). An ANOVA test compares the means of two or more groups. In this example, four groups are being compared. The four groups being compared are the outcomes of each type of promotion. This test will determine if the mean and standard deviation of the individual data sets (by promotion) are significantly different. The actual value of these metrics will identify which one of the promotions drive the highest increase in mean sales.

The outcome of the ANOVA in Excel:

ANOVA: Single Factor

SUMMARY

Groups	Count	Sum	Average	Variance	Std Dev
Spiff	25	376401.40	15056.06	7167692.53	2677.25
Contest	25	434245.20	17369.81	35174536.78	5930.81
5 for 4	25	362230.93	⟨14489.24⟩	2103678.00	1450.41
20% discount	25	278634.63	11145.39	9194086.90	3032.18

The contest drives the highest average sales, whilst the discount drives the least. If the average sales data sets were equal prior to the promotion, then the contest is the most effective promotions.

ANOVA

Source of Variation	SS	df	MS	F	P-value	F crit
Between Groups	494940959.1	3	164980319.7	12.3027843	⟨0.000000704⟩	2.699393
Within Groups	1287359861	96	13409998.55			
Total	1782300820	99				

The p-value reveals a significant difference in sales between the groups (promotions).

The outcome of the ANOVA test reveals that the promotional mean sales level is significantly different depending on the type of promotion. Additionally, the ANOVA identifies, by virtue of the highest mean outcome, that the most successful promotion is the one in which the sales representatives are competing in some contest. Concurrently, the 20 percent discount drove the least impressive sales increase. In fact, these data suggest that both of the promotions that delivered the benefit to the sales representative (the spiff and the contest) drove higher returns than either of the promotions that directed the benefit toward the customer.

With a few quick statistical tests, the project team has proven that promotions do improve average sales, and promotions that benefit sales representatives drive the highest sales increases—at least on the product that was promoted in this study. With this data in hand, the Analyze phase of this project is complete and the task of improving future promotions can be initiated.

IMPROVE

The goal of this project is to prove if promotions have any effect on the sales of a targeted product and to determine which type of promotion is the most effective at increasing sales. Both of these questions were answered in the

Analyze phase. Therefore, the actual structure of the promotion process does not necessarily need to be modified, but which promotion to use does need to be addressed. This project only proved the impact of promotions on whatever product was sold during this experiment. If a company only sells one product and only holds promotions to boost sales, then which promotion to use in the future has been determined. However, if the company is trying to drive different outcomes, such as reduce market erosion or new product introductions, then different types of promotions should be similarly tested If a company sells several different products, then the data from this project may not be valid for all of them. This project could, however, be re-run to evaluate the impact of promotions on other products or other market objectives. If these future project outcomes also show a difference in promotional effectiveness based on product type, then the promotion process could be changed to include a step to "identify the appropriate promotion/product relationship," as shown in Figure 8.8.

If the outcomes were the same, then the initial project finding would have been validated and the project could move to the Control phase.

CONTROL

"Management takes a major step forward when they stop
asking you to explain random variation."

F. Timothy Fuller

The Measure and Analyze steps identified the most useful type of promotions. The Improve step validated these findings and modified the process as necessary. The outcome of the Control phase is to ensure that the improvements that were identified during the project are not lost. Hopefully, the critical functions required to run a promotion (sales and marketing) were included in the original project team. Their participation should facilitate the transfer of ownership for this process from the project team back to the sales and marketing leaders who are ultimately responsible for generating and monitoring promotions. The new process that was developed during the Improve phase should be adapted and followed as the standard operating procedure. Future projects may be launched to further refine these project's conclusions.

Control charts should be used as a visual indication of sales trends and the impact of promotions. This will help to reinforce that the idea that a successful sales promotion is an overall upward sales trend and not just a few high data points. If these control charts accomplish nothing more than to reduce the requests for explanation of individual data points, they will have been successful. Visual displays will also keep the promotion on the minds of the sales and marketing leaders.

The ultimate outcome of this project will be that when the marketing department decides to put together a promotion, the basis for the promotion, the process for the promotion, and the perceived success of the promotion will be based on data and facts, not a gut feeling.

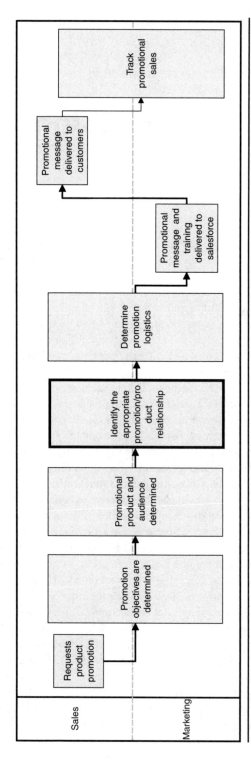

Figure 8.8 Promotion process changed to include "identify the appropriate promotion/product relationship."

9

Conclusion

Six Sigma intends to cultivate fact-based decision-making cultures within the companies that embrace it. It may not resolve every business issue, but Six Sigma offers a problem-solving roadmap that can be applied to any business function.

The successful application of Six Sigma to sales and marketing processes has the potential to be more valuable than in any other business function because transactional processes ultimately drive sales. Improvements to those processes directly generate revenue—something that a manufacturing process cannot claim.

Six Sigma provides the tools to refine these critical processes. The projects in this book represent a few examples of the many opportunities to apply Six Sigma to transactional processes. Even if these projects are not attempted as presented, hopefully this book has opened readers' eyes to the flexibility and potential of Six Sigma. With an expanded awareness of the potential benefits it can create in sales and marketing, Six Sigma can cultivate a stronger reputation within these functions.

To those who previously questioned the benefit of applying a process-driven methodology to transactions that rely on the human element, this author reiterates that Six Sigma was never intended to replicate the magic of the last ten feet of the sale; rather, it is intended to enable that final meeting and improve its likelihood of success. The examples herein demonstrate how Six Sigma can accomplish that goal though a flexible application of its tools and techniques. They also reduce the rule that Six Sigma practitioners attempting to apply their craft to transactional processes must be as flexible as the functions themselves. A rigid application in a flexible environment will be met with resistance and will ultimately impede success.

The ways in which these projects were tackled are certainly not the only ones. Just as there are countless ways to solve a problem without Six Sigma, there are many ways to solve a problem with it. No matter how well-run a business is, problems will arise. Some problems are inherently difficult and will remain so, regardless of the method used to decipher them. After all, if they were simple they would have been resolved long ago. An advantage of using Six Sigma to attack these issues is that Six Sigma challenges teams to systematically *define* the project intent and goal, thus creating an economy of effort. Data will replace hearsay when *measuring* the current capability of the target process. *Analytics* replace gut and supposition in the identification of the root causes. A structured *improvement* process is deployed to test the refined process. Finally, *controls* will be put in place to ensure that what was fixed once will stay that way. If failure comes, fail quickly, gain wisdom from the defeat, and press on with the enlightenment gained. This robust improvement process should be followed on every problem that lacks an obvious solution.

Finally, communication is a key requirement to drive the culture change needed for Six Sigma is to succeed. The CEO must proselytize its value, but the message must be echoed throughout the executive suite. Benefits from Six Sigma efforts should be shared broadly and described in common language, without statistical terms or Six Sigma jargon.

Six Sigma tools in the hands of a business professional are analogous to an artist's tools in the hands of a craftsman. It is in that context that the science of Six Sigma integrates with the art of sales and marketing.

Glossary

alternative hypothesis—A hypothesis that is accepted if the null hypothesis is disproved. Example: Consider the null hypothesis that the statistical model for a population is a normal distribution. The alternative hypothesis to this null hypothesis is that the statistical model of the population is **not** a normal distribution. The alternative hypothesis is a statement that contradicts the null hypothesis. The corresponding test statistic is used to decide between the null and alternative hypotheses.

analysis of variance (ANOVA)—A technique to determine if there are statistically significant differences among group means by analyzing group variances. An ANOVA is an analysis technique that evaluates the importance of several factors of a set of data by subdividing the variation into component parts.

ANOVA tests the hypothesis that the within-group variation is homogeneous and does not vary from group to group. The null hypothesis is that the group means are equal to each other. The alternative hypothesis is that at least one of the group means is different from the others.

attribute—A countable or categorized quality characteristic that is qualitative rather than quantitative in nature. Attribute data come from discrete, nominal, or ordinal scales. Examples of attribute data are irregularities or flaws in a sample and results of pass/fail tests.

average—The central tendency. Common measures are the mean, median, or mode and the calculation depends on the type of distribution. If the term average is used without any descriptor, it is ordinarily the arithmetic mean.

cause-and-effect diagram—A basic tool for analyzing a process; also called Ishikawa diagram or fishbone diagram. The diagram illustrates the main causes and subcauses leading to an effect.

common cause—See random cause.

continuous data—Continuous data is information that can be measured on a continuum or scale. Continuous data can have almost any numeric value and can be meaningfully subdivided into finer and finer increments, depending upon the precision of the measurement system (length, size, width, time, temperature, cost, etc.).

continuous scale—A scale with a continuum of possible values. Note: A continuous scale can be transformed into a discrete scale by grouping values, but this leads to some loss of information.

control chart—A chart that plots a statistical measure of a control series of samples in a particular order to steer Chart Guide the process regarding that measure and to control and reduce variation. Note 1: The order is usually time- or sample number order–based. Note 2: The control chart operates most effectively when the measure is a process characteristic correlated with an ultimate product or service characteristic.

correlation—Correlation measures the linear association between two variables. It is commonly measured by the correlation coefficient, r. See also regression.

Cpk (minimum process capability index)—An index that represents the smaller of CpkU (upper process capability index) and CpkL (lower process capability index).

CpkL (lower process capability index; CPL)—An index describing process capability in relation to the lower specification limit.

CpkU (upper process capability index; CPU)—An index describing process capability in relation to the upper specification

critical to quality (CTQ)—A characteristic of a product or service that is essential to ensure customer satisfaction.

defect—The nonfulfillment of a requirement related to an intended or specified use.

defects per million opportunities (DPMO)—The measure of capability for discrete (attribute) data found by dividing the number of defects by the opportunities for defects times a million. It allows for comparison of different types of product.

defects per unit (DPU)—The measure of capability for discrete (attribute) data found by dividing the number of defects by the number of units.

degrees of freedom (df)—In general, the number of independent comparisons available to estimate a specific parameter that allows entry to certain statistical tables.

discrete scale—A scale with only a set or sequence of distinct values. Examples: Defects per unit, events in a given time period, types of defects, number of orders on a truck.

factor—A predictor variable that is varied with the intent of assessing its effect on a response variable.

flowchart—A basic quality tool that uses graphical representation for the steps in a process. Effective flowcharts include decisions, inputs, and outputs as well as process steps.

frequency—The number of occurrences or observed values in a specified class, sample, or population.

frequency distribution—A set of all the various values that individual observations may have and the frequency of their occurrence in the sample or population.

F-test—A statistical test that uses the F distribution. It is most often used when dealing with a hypothesis related to the ratio of independent variances.

histogram—A plot of a frequency distribution in the form of rectangles (cells) whose bases are equal to the class interval and whose areas are proportional to the frequencies.

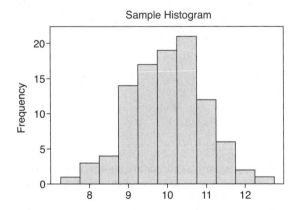

Sample Histogram

hypothesis—A statement about a population to be tested.

hypothesis testing—A statistical hypothesis is a conjecture about a population parameter. There are two statistical hypotheses for each situation—the null hypothesis (H_0) and the alternative hypothesis (H_1). The null hypothesis proposes that there is no difference between the population of the sample and the specified population; the alternative hypothesis proposes that there is a difference between the sample and the specified population.

in-control process—A condition where the existence of special causes is no longer present. It indicates (within limits) a predictable and stable process, but it does not indicate that only random causes remain; nor does it imply that the distribution of the remaining values is normal.

independent variable—An independent variable is an input or process variable (X) that can be set directly to achieve a desired output.

input variable—A variable that can contribute to the variation in a process.

Ishikawa diagram—See cause-and-effect diagram.

least squares, method of—A technique of estimating a parameter that minimizes the sum of the difference squared, where the difference is between the observed value and the predicted value (residual) derived from the model. The usual analysis of variance, regression analysis, and analysis of covariance are all based on the method of least squares.

linear regression equation—A function that indicates the linear relationship between a set of predictor variables and a response variable.

μ (mu)—See population mean.

mean—The mean is the average data point value within a data set. To calculate the mean, add all of the individual data points then divide that figure by the total number of data points

median—The value for which half the data is larger and half is smaller. The median provides an estimator that is insensitive to very extreme values in a data set, whereas the average is affected by extreme values. Note: For an odd number of units, the median is the middle measurement; for an even number of units, the median is the average of the two middle measurements.

mode—The most frequent value of a variable in a sample or population.

multiple linear regression—Multiple regression is a method of determining the relationship between a continuous process output (Y) and several factors (Xs).

n—The number of units in a size.

nominal scale—A scale with unordered, labeled categories, or a scale ordered by convention. Examples: Type of defect, breed of dog, complaint category. Note: It is possible to count by category, but not order or measure.

normal distribution (Gaussian distribution)—A continuous, symmetrical frequency distribution that produces a bell-shaped curve. The location parameter (x-axis) is the mean, m. The scale parameter, s, is the standard deviation of the normal distribution. When measurements have a normal distribution, 68.26% of the values lie within plus or minus one standard deviation of the mean; 95.44% lie within plus or minus two standard deviations of the mean; while 99.73% lie within plus or minus three standard deviations of the mean.

null hypothesis, H_0—The hypothesis in tests of significance that there is no difference (null) between the population of the sample and the specified population (or between the populations associated with each sample). The null hypothesis can never be proved true, but it can be shown (with specified risks or error) to be untrue; that is, a difference exists between the populations. If it is not disproved, one assumes there is no adequate reason to doubt it is true, and the null hypothesis is accepted. If the null hypothesis is shown to be untrue, then the alternative hypothesis is accepted. Example: In a random sample of independent random variables with the same normal distribution with unknown mean and unknown standard deviation, a typical null hypothesis for the mean, μ, is that the mean is less than or equal to a given value, μ_0.

one-tailed test—A hypothesis test that involves only one of the tails of a distribution. A one-tailed test is either right-tailed or left-tailed, depending on the direction of the inequality of the alternative hypothesis.

ordinal scale—A scale with ordered, labeled categories.

outlier—An extremely high or an extremely low data value compared to the rest of the data values. Great caution must be used when trying to identify an outlier.

output variable—The variable representing the outcome of the *process*.

Pareto chart—A graphical tool based on the Pareto principle for ranking causes from most significant to least significant.

Pareto principle—The principle, named after 19th century economist Vilfredo Pareto, suggests that most effects come from relatively few causes; that is, about 80 percent of effects come from about 20 percent of the possible causes.

Pearson's correlation coefficient—reflects the degree of linear relationship between two variables. Pearson's correlation coefficient (r) for continuous (interval level) data ranges from -1 to +1. Positive correlation indicates that both variables increase or decrease together, whereas negative correlation indicates that as one variable increases, so the other decreases, and vice versa.

population—The entire set (totality) of units, quantity of material, or observations under consideration. A population may be real and finite, real and infinite, or completely hypothetical.

population mean (μ)—The true mean of the population, represented by μ (mu). The sample mean, x, is a common estimator of the population mean.

predictor variable—A variable that can contribute to the explanation of the outcome of an experiment.

probability (P)—The chance of an event occurring.

probability distribution—A function that completely describes the probabilities with which specific values occur. The values may be from a discrete scale or a continuous scale.

process—A series of interrelated steps consisting of resources and activities that transform inputs into outputs and work together to a common end. A process can be graphically represented using a flowchart.

process capability—The calculated inherent variability of a characteristic of a product. It represents the best performance of the process over a period of stable operations

process capability index—A single-number assessment of ability to meet specification limits on the quality characteristic(s) of interest. The indices compare the variability of the characteristic to the specification limits. Three basic process capability indices are Cp, Cpk, and Cpm.

process control—is the methodology for keeping a process within boundaries and minimizing the variation of a process.

process performance—The statistical measure of the outcome of a characteristic from a process that may not have been demonstrated to be in a state of statistical control. Note: Use this measure cautiously since it may contain a component of variability from special causes of unpredictable value. It differs from process capability because a state of statistical control is not required.

p-value—The probability value (p-value) of a statistical hypothesis test is the probability of getting a value of the test statistic as extreme as or more extreme than that observed by chance alone, if the null hypothesis H_0, is true.

random cause—The source of process variation that is inherent in a process over time. Also called common cause or chance cause. Note: In a process subject only to random cause variation, the variation is predictable within statistically established limits.

random sampling—A sampling where a sample of n sampling units is taken from a population in such a way that each of the possible combinations of n sampling units has a particular probability of being taken.

random variation—Variation from random causes.

randomization—The process used to assign treatments to experimental units so that each experimental unit has an equal chance of being assigned a particular treatment. Randomization validates the assumptions made in statistical analysis and prevents unknown biases from impacting the conclusions.

regression analysis—A technique that uses predictor variable(s) to predict the variation in a response variable. Regression analysis uses the method of least squares to determine the values of the linear regression coefficients and the corresponding model. It is particularly pertinent when the predictor variables are continuous and emphasis is on creating a predictive model. When some of the predictor variables are discrete, analysis of variance or analysis of covariance is likely a more appropriate method. This resulting model can then test the resulting predictions for statistical significance against an appropriate null hypothesis model. The model also gives some sense of the degree of linearity present in the data. When only one predictor variable is used, regression analysis is often referred to as simple linear regression. A simple linear regression model commonly uses a linear regression equation expressed as $Y = mx + b$, where Y is the response, x is the value of the predictor variable. b is often called the intercept and m is often called the slope. When multiple predictor variables are used, regression is referred to as multiple linear regression. The multiple regression equation takes the form $y = b1 \times 1 + b2 \times 2 + ... + bnxn + c$. The b's are the regression coefficients, representing the amount the dependent variable y changes when the corresponding independent changes 1 unit. The c is the constant, where the regression line intercepts the y axis, representing the amount the dependent y will be when all the independent variables are 0. The standardized version of the b coefficients are the beta weights, and the ratio of the beta coefficients is the ratio of the relative predictive power of the independent variables The random error terms in regression analysis are often assumed to be normally distributed with a constant variance. These assumptions can be readily checked through residual analysis or residual plots.

root cause analysis—The process of identifying causes. Many systems are available for analyzing data to ultimately determine the root cause.

sigma—The Greek letter s (sigma) refers to the standard deviation of a population. Sigma, or standard deviation, is used as a scaling factor to convert upper and lower specification limits to Z. Therefore, a process with three standard deviations between its mean and a spec limit would have a Z value of 3 and commonly would be referred to as a 3 sigma process.

sample—A group of units, portions or material, or observations taken from a larger collection of units, quantity of material, or observations that serves to provide information that may be used for making a decision concerning the larger quantity (the population).

Note 1: The sample may be the actual units or material or the observations collected from them. The decision may or may not involve taking action on the units or material, or on the process.

Note 2: Sampling plans are schemes set up statistically in order to provide a sampling system with minimum bias.

Note 3: There are many different ways, random and nonrandom, to select a sample. In survey sampling, sampling units are often selected with a probability proportional to the size of a known variable, giving a biased sample.

significance level—The maximum probability of rejecting the null hypothesis when in fact it is true. Note: The significance level is usually designated by α and should be set before beginning the test.

significance tests—Significance tests are a method of deciding, with certain predetermined risks of error, (1) whether the population associated with a sample differs from the one specified; (2) whether the population associated with each of two samples differ; or (3) whether the populations associated with each of more than two samples differ. Significance testing is equivalent to the testing of hypotheses. Therefore, a clear statement of the null hypothesis, alternative hypotheses, and predetermined selection of a confidence level are required.

simple linear regression—See regression analysis.

Six Sigma—Six Sigma is a rigorous and a systematic methodology that utilizes information (management by facts) and statistical analysis to measure and improve a company's operational performance, practices and systems by identifying and preventing 'defects' in manufacturing and service-related processes.

skewness—A measure of symmetry about the mean. For a normal distribution, skewness is zero because the distribution is symmetric.

slope—See regression analysis.

special cause—A source of process variation other than inherent process variation.

special cause variation—Special cause variation is a shift in output caused by a specific factor such as environmental conditions or process input parameters. It can be accounted for directly and potentially removed and is a measure of process control.

spread—The spread of a process represents how far data points are distributed away from the mean, or center. Standard deviation is a measure of spread.

stable process—A process that is predictable within limits; a process that is subject only to random causes. (This is also known as a state of statistical control.)

Note 1: A stable process will generally behave as though the results are simple random samples from the same population.

Note 2: This state does not imply that the random variation is large or small, within or outside of specification limits, but rather that the variation is predictable using statistical techniques.

Note 3: The process capability of a stable process is usually improved by fundamental changes that reduce or remove some of the random causes present and/or adjusting the mean toward the target value.

standard deviation—A measure of the spread of the process output or the spread of a sampling statistic from the process. When working with the population, the standard deviation is usually denoted by σ (sigma). When working with a sample the standard deviation is usually denoted by s.

statistic—A quantity calculated from a sample of observations, most often to form an estimate of some population parameter.

statistical measure—A statistic or mathematical function of a statistic.

statistical process control (SPC)—The use of statistical techniques such as control charts to reduce variation, increase knowledge about the process, and to steer the process in the desired way.

Note 1: SPC operates most efficiently by controlling variation of the process or inprocess characteristics that correlate with a final product characteristic and/or by increasing the robustness of the process against this variation.

Note 2: A supplier's final product characteristic can be a process characteristic of the next downstream supplier's process.

statistical thinking—A philosophy of learning and action based on the following fundamental principles:

- All work occurs in a system of interconnected processes.

- Variation exists in all processes.

- Understanding and reducing variation are keys to success.

subgroup—A distinct group within a group; a subdivision or subset of a group.

t-**test**—A test for significance that uses the t distribution to compare a sample statistic to a hypothesized population mean or to compare two means. See t-test (one sample), t-test (two-sample), t-test (paired data).

Note: Testing the equality of the means of two normal populations with unknown but equal variances can be extended to the comparison of k population means. This test procedure is called analysis of variance (ANOVA).

t-**test (one-sample)**—A test for significance where is the mean of the data is the hypothesized population mean.

t-**test (paired data)**—Samples are paired to eliminate differences between specimens. The test could involve two machines, two test methods, two treatments, and so on. Observations are the pairs of the two machines, tests, treatments, and so on. The differences of the pairs of observations on each of the *n* specimens

t-**test (two-sample)**—When there are two populations with unknown Equal variances means and unknown variances that are assumed to be equal.

two-tailed test—A hypothesis test that involves tails of a distribution. In a two tailed test, direction is unimportant. Example: We wish to reject the null hypothesis if the true mean is within minimum and maximum (two tails) limits.

Type I error—The probability or risk of rejecting a hypothesis that is true. This probability is represented by a (alpha).

Type II error—The probability or risk of accepting a hypothesis that is false. This probability is represented by b (beta). See diagram below.

unit—A quantity of product, material, or service forming a cohesive entity on which a measurement or observation can be made.

variance—A measure of the variation in the data. When working with the entire population, the population variance is used; when working with a sample, the sample variance is used. The population variance is based on the mean of the squared deviations from the arithmetic

	H_0 True	H_0 False
Do not reject H_0	Correct decision	Error Type II
Reject H_0	Error Type I	Correct decision

mean. The sample variance is based on the squared deviations from the arithmetic mean divided by n–1.

variances, tests for—A formal statistical test based on the null hypothesis that the variances of different groups are equal. Many times in regression analysis a formal test of variances is not done. Instead, residual analysis checks the assumption of equal variance across the values of the response variable in the model. For two variances, see F-test.

variation—The difference between values of a characteristic. Variation can be measured and calculated in different ways, such as range, standard deviation, or variance. Also known as dispersion or spread.

VOC—Voice of the customer. The "voice of the customer" is the term used to describe the stated and unstated needs of the customer. The voice of the customer can be captured in a variety of ways: direct discussion or interviews, surveys, focus groups, customer specifications, observation, warranty data, field reports, complaint logs, etc.

Z-Table—Entries in the body of the table represents areas under the normal curve between $-\infty$ and z.

	0.00	0.01	0.02	0.03	0.04	0.05	0.06	0.07	0.08	0.09
0.0	0.5000	0.5040	0.5080	0.5120	0.5160	0.5199	0.5239	0.5279	0.5319	0.5359
0.1	0.5398	0.5438	0.5478	0.5517	0.5557	0.5596	0.5636	0.5675	0.5714	0.5753
0.2	0.5793	0.5832	0.5871	0.5910	0.5948	0.5987	0.6026	0.6064	0.6103	0.6141
0.3	0.6179	0.6217	0.6255	0.6293	0.6331	0.6368	0.6406	0.6443	0.6480	0.6517
0.4	0.6554	0.6591	0.6628	0.6664	0.6700	0.6736	0.6772	0.6808	0.6844	0.6879
0.5	0.6915	0.6950	0.6985	0.7019	0.7054	0.7088	0.7123	0.7157	0.7190	0.7224
0.6	0.7257	0.7291	0.7324	0.7357	0.7389	0.7422	0.7454	0.7486	0.7517	0.7549
0.7	0.7580	0.7611	0.7642	0.7673	0.7704	0.7734	0.7764	0.7794	0.7823	0.7852
0.8	0.7881	0.7910	0.7939	0.7967	0.7995	0.8023	0.8051	0.8078	0.8106	0.8133
0.9	0.8159	0.8186	0.8212	0.8238	0.8264	0.8289	0.8315	0.8340	0.8365	0.8389
1.0	0.8413	0.8438	0.8461	0.8485	0.8508	0.8531	0.8554	0.8577	0.8599	0.8621
1.1	0.8643	0.8665	0.8686	0.8708	0.8729	0.8749	0.8770	0.8790	0.8810	0.8830
1.2	0.8849	0.8869	0.8888	0.8907	0.8925	0.8944	0.8962	0.8980	0.8997	0.9015
1.3	0.9032	0.9049	0.9066	0.9082	0.9099	0.9115	0.9131	0.9147	0.9162	0.9177
1.4	0.9192	0.9207	0.9222	0.9236	0.9251	0.9265	0.9279	0.9292	0.9306	0.9319
1.5	0.9332	0.9345	0.9357	0.9370	0.9382	0.9394	0.9406	0.9418	0.9429	0.9441
1.6	0.9452	0.9463	0.9474	0.9484	0.9495	0.9505	0.9515	0.9525	0.9535	0.9545
1.7	0.9554	0.9564	0.9573	0.9582	0.9591	0.9599	0.9608	0.9616	0.9625	0.9633
1.8	0.9641	0.9649	0.9656	0.9664	0.9671	0.9678	0.9686	0.9693	0.9699	0.9706
1.9	0.9713	0.9719	0.9726	0.9732	0.9738	0.9744	0.9750	0.9756	0.9761	0.9767
2.0	0.9772	0.9778	0.9783	0.9788	0.9793	0.9798	0.9803	0.9808	0.9812	0.9817
2.1	0.9821	0.9826	0.9830	0.9834	0.9838	0.9842	0.9846	0.9850	0.9854	0.9857
2.2	0.9861	0.9864	0.9868	0.9871	0.9875	0.9878	0.9881	0.9884	0.9887	0.9890
2.3	0.9893	0.9896	0.9898	0.9901	0.9904	0.9906	0.9909	0.9911	0.9913	0.9916
2.4	0.9918	0.9920	0.9922	0.9925	0.9927	0.9929	0.9931	0.9932	0.9934	0.9936
2.5	0.9938	0.9940	0.9941	0.9943	0.9945	0.9946	0.9948	0.9949	0.9951	0.9952
2.6	0.9953	0.9955	0.9956	0.9957	0.9959	0.9960	0.9961	0.9962	0.9963	0.9964
2.7	0.9965	0.9966	0.9967	0.9968	0.9969	0.9970	0.9971	0.9972	0.9973	0.9974
2.8	0.9974	0.9975	0.9976	0.9977	0.9977	0.9978	0.9979	0.9979	0.9980	0.9981
2.9	0.9981	0.9982	0.9982	0.9983	0.9984	0.9984	0.9985	0.9985	0.9986	0.9986
3.0	0.9987	0.9987	0.9987	0.9988	0.9988	0.9989	0.9989	0.9989	0.9990	0.9990

Index